The Author

HAROLD E. HATT is professor of theology and philosophy, The Graduate Seminary, Phillips University, Enid, Oklahoma.

He is a graduate of the University of British Columbia (B.A.) Southwestern Baptist Theological Seminary (B.D.), Baylor University (M.A.), and Vanderbilt University (Ph.D.).

Dr. Hatt served the Carthage (Tennessee) Christian Church and taught at North Texas State University, Denton, Texas, before joining the Phillips faculty in 1962.

He completed his Ph.D. work at Vanderbilt on a Rockefeller Doctoral Fellowship. He is a member of the American Academy of Religion and the American Philosophical Association.

S0-BAQ-367

Encountering Truth

Encountering Truth

A New Understanding of How Revelation as Encounter Yields Doctrine

by Harold E. Hatt

Abingdon Press • Nashville • New York

ENCOUNTERING TRUTH

Copyright © 1966 by Abingdon Press

Library of Congress Catalog Card Number: 66-22917

SET UP, PRINTED, AND BOUND BY THE
PARTHENON PRESS, AT NASHVILLE,
TENNESSEE, UNITED STATES OF AMERICA

To My Wife, Martha

Contents

1. Revelation as Encounter and the Problem of Doctrine

The concept of revelation, and especially the problem of its relation to reason, has had a fascination for theologians throughout the history of Christian thought. But even though the concept of revelation has received very persistent and very concentrated attention, contemporary theology has introduced a startling new chapter into the history of the interpretation of revelation. How can one conceive of the process of revelation as anything other than the imparting of knowledge or information? How can the content of revelation be anything other than knowledge in the form of propositions or statements which affirm truths? Yet it is this very limitation of the propositional framework that has been superseded. In the past men have held widely varying opinions on such issues as how revelation is imparted, whether its content is simple or complex, whether faith precedes, follows, or coincides with reason. Such issues as these caused theological divisions, but until the modern period everybody from scholastics to deists, from pietists to rationalists operated within the "information barrier."

Encounter theology affirms and seeks to elaborate the understanding of revelation as lying beyond the "information barrier." Encounter theology draws upon the concept of "I-Thou" encounter as a central category in its comprehension and exposition of the Christian faith. Revelation is understood to be the personal self-disclosure of God to man, not the impartation of truths about God. Doctrines are the result of later rational reflection upon the self-manifestation of God, but they distort the encounter with God because they are in the sphere of I-It rather than I-Thou. Encounter theologians emphatically contend that this contemporary concept of I-Thou encounter between God and man is simply a rediscovery of the basic point of view in the Bible (although they also discern a movement away from this perspective at various points in the Bible). For encounter theology the "information barrier" is not a natural one, which we have just recently surpassed, but one which man erected and imposed on himself and which he has now come to understand was spurious. Propositional theology, having roots in American fundamentalism and Reformed orthodoxy on the continent, has staunchly retained the traditional understanding of revelation as the impartation of propositions, and conceives of the theological task as that of systematizing revealed truths. According to propositional theology the breaking of the "information barrier" is a denial of the biblical witness; according to encounter theology it is a reappropriation of the biblical witness.

Encounter theology has now reached a point of maturity at which examination of its foundations is both possible and necessary. It has been attacked from both right and left and has conducted itself admirably on both fronts. Its success in the heat of theological controversy does not mean that encounter theology can retire from the demands of life, but rather that it is time for a new self-appraisal. Many have expressed the need for clarification of the relation between doctrine and

10

revelation as personal encounter with God. The problem is very sensitive indeed. If no knowledge is revealed in encounter, and if any objective understanding of encounter is a distortion and perversion, then how does revelation give rise to theological knowledge about God? I am convinced that this problem is not only deserving of new attention but that any detailed examination of this question must move the issue into a new phase. Specifically, the new phase that seems to me to be inevitable is that encounter theology must recognize I-It elements in the divine-human encounter as well as in the encounter between men. I believe that this recognition would not weaken encounter theology but would strengthen it by clarifying the relation between revelation and doctrine.

Clarification of the nature of revelation is imperative because this concept is central in contemporary theology. Baillie points out, in the preface to the series of essays gathered under the title *Revelation*, that not only discussions of faith and order but also of life and work and of the missionary enterprise have called for a more thorough discussion of the problem of revelation.

> It would appear . . . that the topic of revelation is the first order of urgency as regards the Church's total task in the present age. . . . Indeed, if one were asked what was, just at the present moment, the most frequented hunting ground of the theologians, one would have to answer without hesitation that it was the doctrine of revelation—a sufficiently remarkable contrast to the situation obtaining in, say, the years immediately prior to the Great War.[1]

Since the doctrine of revelation is a frequented "hunting ground" in contemporary theology, this study stakes out a nar-

---

[1] John Baillie and Hugh Martin, eds. (New York: Macmillan, 1937), pp. x-xi. For a more recent treatment of the doctrine of revelation, see the brief but excellent survey in John Baillie's *The Idea of Revelation in Recent Thought* (New York: Columbia University Press, 1956).

rowly confined area of investigation. There is no attempt to respond to those who would deny the being of God nor the possibility of genuine (nonillusory) relationship with him. These challenges raise problems which are vitally significant to theology, but they are considered to lie beyond the scope of the present work, which presupposes the possibility of a relationship with God that is not simply a projection or some other form of delusion. To state the issue positively, the concern of this study is restricted to an evaluation of how revelation as encounter and revelation as propositional are understood as sources of doctrinal material, and an examination of a view which is considered to be a more accurate description of the relation between revelation and doctrine.

The understanding of how revelation yields doctrine that is proposed here is compatible with the current emphasis on the epistemological transcendence of God and of the consequent necessity of revelation. We know God only through his own act of disclosure. God is not someone whom we find by our own efforts. We cannot discover God through doctrines, through theistic proofs, through natural theology, through ethical maxims, and so forth. We are dependent upon his own act of self-manifestation. However, it is a distortion to stop at this point. One of the major reasons for the epistemological transcendence of God is his ontological transcendence. Revelation is essential to our knowledge of God because the being of God is not like the being of man and the world. God is self-sufficient being; we have contingent being. Because God's being is different from our own being and from the being of the things we know, there is no way for us to discover God; he must disclose himself to us. Consequently, the affirmation that God is epistemologically transcendent, so that there is no knowledge of him apart from revelation, in no way obviates ontology. Rather, it presupposes an ontology.

Furthermore, transcendence and immanence are polar concepts, and it is impossible to eliminate one by means of the other. A completely transcendent God would be utterly unknowable and we would have no basis for employing the phrase "wholly other" of a completely transcendent deity. Even if we were to imagine such an utterly transcendent God making his nature known, a completely nonimmanent God would be quite irrelevant. Gilkey makes this point vividly:

He might, it is true, enter like an invader from Mars into our world, as an interesting addition to the things that are in it. But surely if he is thus irrelevant to the essential ongoing of the world, it would be absurd to say that the world had been "lost" without him, or "saved" by his new presence in its midst.[2]

There may be no saving knowledge of God apart from revelation, but there is no salvation unless God is immanent. We may not discover God on the basis of his immanence but, having found God in Christ, we find the God who is the source and sustainer of all things. Consequently, having seen God first in Christ, we then find him immanent in all reality.

An example of both the strengths and weaknesses of the rediscovery of the personal basis of theology is found in Gustaf Aulén. His work throughout illustrates the vitality of the new emphasis on God's epistemological transcendence, but also its tendency to obscure the theological significance of God's ontological transcendence and immanence. These shortcomings are illustrated in these statements:

The reason systematic theology does not want to have any part with rational metaphysics is not simply because such a metaphysic is suspect from a critical point of view. . . . The reason is rather that faith has really nothing to do with rationalistic metaphysics.

[2] Langdon Gilkey, *Maker of Heaven and Earth* (Garden City, N.Y.: Doubleday, 1959), p. 96.

Once faith has found God in Christ it does not seek him elsewhere.[3]

The nature of faith as a trustful commitment to a redeeming personal God is an important emphasis, but it is undergirded, rather than undermined, by the categories of such disciplines as metaphysics and science. In support of this contention, the emendation that is attempted in this study describes man's relation to God as basically an I-Thou relation which nonetheless includes I-It elements as essential to encounter.

Contemporary theology has exerted tremendous energy and zeal in its reappropriation of the emphasis of Reformation theology on the personal confrontation of God and man. For example, the chapter entitled "The Name of God" in Emil Brunner's *The Christian Doctrine of God* is not a tedious recital of and commentary on the various appellations that have been used of deity. Rather, it is an exciting presentation of God's nature as personal. A similar emphasis is found in H. Richard Niebuhr's *The Meaning of Revelation* which, with its appreciation of the impact of historical relativism on contemporary thought, makes an eloquent appeal for the understanding of revelation as the disclosure through history of a personal God. And the reader can no doubt multiply these examples.

But in addition to the traditions of encounter and propositional theology there is another vital tradition in contemporary theology. Stemming largely from the work of Paul Tillich, this tradition argues that personal imagery is inadequate for speaking of God. For Tillich it is not enough to say that God is a "thou" whom we confront. God must rather be understood as the "ground of being" and only ontological terms are adequate for speaking of God.

And so we have a theological tug-of-war. This is not a par-

---

[3] Gustaf Aulén, *The Faith of the Christian Church,* tr. by Eric H. Wahlstrom (Philadelphia: Muhlenberg, 1960), pp. 11, 54.

ticularly unusual situation for theology, and there are times when one should get on one end of the rope or other and tug. But in this particular controversy I am convinced that these two forces should be pulling together instead of against each other. The argument of this book is that I-Thou encounter with God necessarily contains I-It elements, and we have already considered some of the shortcomings of an exclusive personalism. It is hoped that the thesis of this book may provide a rationale for the necessary use of both personal and ontological imagery in speaking of God.

Although the ontological thought of Paul Tillich is not directly examined in this study, it is very much in the background. My own response to Tillich differs from that of Brunner, and it reflects the emendation of encounter theology that is proposed in this book. This is an age in which the personal dimension is difficult for people to comprehend and appreciate. In his response to Tillich, Brunner alludes to this spirit of the age and commends Tillich's attempt to meet modern man where he is, even at the risk of distorting the biblical witness which is "starkly personalistic." Brunner rejects Tillich's ontological analysis but commends his apologetic witness. Tillich's "function is eminently missionary, indeed precisely by virtue of what we must reject on theological grounds." [4] I concur heartily with Brunner's respect for the apologetic value of Tillich's theology. However, I do not consider ontological analysis *per se* to be a distortion of the "starkly personalistic" biblical witness. Rather I welcome it as a necessary and vital aspect of the theological task. On the other hand, I disagree with Tillich's insistence that the personalism of neo-Reformation theology needs to give way to ontological categories. I appreciate Tillich's apologetic concern, but I do not consider it incompatible

---

[4] H. Emil Brunner, "Reply to Interpretation and Criticism" in *The Theology of Emil Brunner*, Charles W. Kegley, ed. (New York: Macmillan, 1962), p. 335.

with the emphasis of encounter theology. And yet we need a rationale for this combination of contending theological traditions, and one of the aims of this book is to provide such justification.

Ontology *per se* is not destructive of biblical personalism. I have already indicated that the assertion of God's epistemological transcendence implicates one in ontology. Yet impersonal, ontological imagery does seem to be inimical to encounter and dialogue. But this is not the fault of ontological thought and impersonal imagery. Rather, it is due to our insensitivity to the personal dimension.

"Encounter" and "dialogue" are terms that have become faddish, and many of those who mouth them as cure-alls have not really understood them. This is illustrated in those who are so convinced of the value of free give-and-take dialogue and encounter that they will program it so as to force it upon other people who "need" it. Instead of a spontaneous relation, respecting the freedom and individuality of the other, dialogue has become a technique for manipulating others, and in reality the I-Thou is replaced by the I-It.

When we enter into personal relation, we are confronting another free and independent personality. If we try to manipulate the other person, we are not relating to him as a thou but as an it. This does not mean that the other person's will is inevitably in conflict with our own, though Sartre makes a strong case for this. But we are always aware of a potential conflict of interest. Even though the other is beyond our control, there is nonetheless a community of values on which a personal relation can be built. The situation is well described by H. H. Farmer as a polarity of "value-cooperation" and "value-resistance." [5]

But, to turn to the other point, I contend that the apologetic

[5] H. H. Farmer, *The World and God* (New York: Harper & Brothers, 1936), p. 22.

task may be better carried out by cultivating man's sensitivity to the personal dimension in life. There is no question that this dimension is difficult for our contemporaries. It is being commendably "honest to God" [6] to point out that the traditional language of transcendence is irrelevant to most of our contemporaries, both Christian and non-Christian. But this opens, not closes, the question of the appropriate Christian witness in our age. Should personal imagery be subordinated or rehabilitated? To de-emphasize personal imagery in theology seems to be succumbing to the modern age rather than witnessing to it. I would suggest that to cultivate man's awareness of the personal dimension is much more "honest to God," even for one who is convinced that this is hardly the starting point or point of contact.

The process which Karl Marx described as *Verdinglichung* has grown apace since his day. It is not simply that men have become things because others have so treated them, but also because they have so treated others. Men need to be called to task of thinking in terms of the personal dimension of life, not relieved of this responsibility.

The concept of the personal can incorporate the lower dimensions. To supplement personal with impersonal imagery seems to be a preferable way to make the same essential gain that Tillich makes by subsuming the personal within the suprapersonal. In describing how nature can become revelatory Tillich says: "There is no difference between a stone and a person in their potentiality of becoming bearers of revelation by entering a revelatory constellation. But there is a great difference between them with respect to the significance and truth of the revelations mediated through them." [7]

[6] John A. T. Robinson, *Honest to God* (Philadelphia: Westminster, 1963. See especially chaps. 2-3 and 7.

[7] Paul Tillich, *Systematic Theology* (Chicago: University of Chicago Press, 1951), I, 118.

Tillich goes on to assert that despite its limitations the stone is able to express qualities that cannot be represented by a person, and he cites enduring and resisting as examples. But is this really so? When we think of a person as enduring or resisting, are we really attributing qualities of a stone to them in a metaphorical sense which we could not understand in personal terms alone? And even if the answer should be yes, which I doubt, have we not shown at least that the personal can incorporate the impersonal? The fullest sympathy with the intention not to limit God by describing him as "a person" does not necessitate the subordinating of personal imagery for speaking of God. We do not encounter God as "a person," but we do encounter him as personal—and the personal qualities are basic and central, even though they may need to be completed by the impersonal categories of ontology.

This discussion is not intended as a full-fledged defense of the use of personal imagery, but simply as an introduction to this investigation of how revelation yields doctrine. A full-fledged defense of the use of personal imagery would need to examine further such things as the concomitant increase of mystery and knowledge of God *(deus revelatus est deus absconditus)* and the analogy with our knowledge of persons, the final revelation of God through the medium of personal incarnation, the need of an accompanying word to interpret the mighty acts of God, and so forth. But our purpose here is simply to indicate briefly how the proposed emendation of encounter theology is able to overcome the tug-of-war between personal and ontological imagery. If it has succeeded in indicating this, we can now turn our attention to the examination of encounter theology, propositional theology, and a new understanding of how revelation yields doctrine.

The procedure of this book is to investigate and evaluate the concepts of revelation as encounter and as propositional. It is concluded that a more adequate understanding of revelation is achieved by an emendation of encounter theology to include I-It elements in the divine-human encounter. This is in contrast with the relegation of I-It knowledge to a distinct sphere, as in the unemended form of encounter theology, and with the elevation of assent so that it absorbs trust, as in propositional theology. The inclusion of I-It elements in divine-human encounter provides a basis for the inclusion of ontological terminology in theological discourse.

The specific focus of this work is upon the question: "How does revelation yield doctrine?" Assuming that there is a God who makes himself known to man, I want to address myself to the problem of how this relation to God yields doctrinal material. My contention is that we are not given an adequate answer either by those who consider revelation to be the disclosure of propositions or by those who understand revelation as encounter.

Encounter theology, represented by Martin Buber and Emil Brunner, contends that God reveals himself not through propositions but through personal presence, and that knowledge about God is not essential to relation with him. Doctrines are not revealed but are the result of subsequent rational reflection upon encounter and are always a distortion of it, in the sense of being an intellectual abstraction of that which cannot be expressed adequately in intellectual terms.

Propositional theology, represented by J. Gresham Machen, B. B. Warfield, and Abraham Kuyper, contends that God reveals himself through propositions which are infallibly recorded in the Bible. Human reason extracts the system of theology in the Bible, and faith is understood as assenting to the truth of revealed doctrines and trusting God on the basis of them.

Chapters 2-4 deal with encounter theology. Because the concept of "encounter" has become so well-known, it is considered rather briefly. Our major concern in this study is not the encounter between man and man but between God and man, and with the concept of revelation that emerges from this theological perspective. It is argued that encounter theology fails to establish the analogy of encounter. In order to distinguish between encounter with persons and with God, encounter theologians considered the latter to be completely free of I-It elements (a "pure" encounter with one who is always "Thou," never "It"). However, the impossibility of establishing a scale of purity-impurity for encounter renders this principle incapable of pointing in the direction of divine-human encounter. It is also argued that encounter theology has difficulty in maintaining a sharp dichotomy between trust in a person and assent to propositions about a person, and several concessions to the significance of assent are noted.

Chapters 5-6 examine propositional theology. In light of the shortcomings of encounter theology, the option of propositional theology merits reexamination. The encounter theologians' charge that propositional theologians are bibliolaters is upheld, but it is observed that the charge itself implies the theological significance of I-It knowledge. The insistence of propositional theology on the revelation of infallible propositions is adjudged untenable and incapable of emendation. However, the value of the emphasis on the objective element in revelation is influential on the suggested explanation of how revelation yields doctrine.

Chapter 7 returns to encounter theology, with a view to emending it in the light of the criticism of that position in Chapters 2-4 and the criticism of an alternative position in Chapters 5-6. The first task is to provide a new basis for the analogy of encounter to replace the untenable basis that there is a scale of purity-impurity in encounter, pointing to divine-human encounter which is prefectly pure of I-It elements. The contrast between the infinitude of God and the finitude of man is considered as a principle of successfully distinguishing divine-human encounter from encounter between men. This new principle of modification allows for a more adequate understanding of revelation by making it possible to include I-It elements within divine-human encounter, just as they are already recognized as present in encounter between man and man.

The basic thesis of this book is that there is an existential, personal type of knowledge present in divine-human encounter. In support of this proposal consideration is given to the nature of language as an expression of both feeling and knowledge and to the involvement of knowledge in every emotional state. The occurrence of "nonveridical encounters" is discussed as demonstrating the role of interpretation within encounter. It is argued that our sense of relation and interpretation of it are inseparable elements of encounter, and that without interpretation there could be no recognition of "I" and "Thou" or any basis for mutual self-giving. It is contended that this existential, personal type of knowledge is operative prior to, within, and subsequent to the encounter itself. The existential, personal type of knowledge present in encounter is not infallibly communicated but is received through human interpretation. It is not doctrine but a source of doctrine. It is later elaborated into doctrine along with knowledge gained through the cumulative witness of the church, rational reflection upon the encounter, and other rational activities, such as science and philosophy.

2. Buber and Brunner:
Encounter and God

The publication of *I and Thou* came with first a dazzling and soon a revolutionary impact upon the contemporary world of thought. It is written in a fashion which has been described as *un peu dramatique mais pourtant juste*[1]—an understatement which is more typical of the British than of the Gallic mind. The seemingly narrow scope of this work proved to be a misleading feature, as its influence reached out to pervade more and more of thought. Buber's

thinking has the narrowness and concrete power, often the stubborn obstinacy, of Hebraism. At first glance his contribution would seem to be the slenderest of all the Existentialists. . . . It is as if Buber had sought to recast Kierkegaard's dictum, "Purity of heart is to will one thing," into: Depth of mind is to think one

[1] Roger Mehl, *La condition du philosophe Chrétien* (Neuchâtel: Delachaux & Niestlé, 1947, p. 82 n. Buber sketched this work in 1916, wrote it in 1919, and published it in 1923. Page references are to: Martin Buber, *I and Thou*, tr. by Ronald Gregor Smith (Edinburgh: T. & T. Clark, 1937). The 2nd ed. (New York: Scribner's, 1958) has two verbal changes in translation and has a "Postscript" by Buber.

thought. But this one thought—that meaning in life happens in the area between person and person in that situation of contact when one says *I* to the other's *Thou*—is worth a lifetime's digging.[2]

Hans Urs von Balthasar also notes the combination of simplicity and force in Buber. He remarks that "Buber's method is one of ruthless simplification and clarification in which everything superfluous or inessential is mercilessly swept aside." [3] The best known of Buber's categories is his distinction between "I-Thou" and "I-It." In this study we are primarily concerned with Buber's development and elaboration of this point of view in his discussion of our knowledge of God. However, before we give attention to his concept of God as the eternal Thou and the nature of our knowledge of God, we can profit from a more general consideration of this basis of Buber's thought.

Buber's distinction between I-It and I-Thou soon made its influence felt within Christian theology, where it has served as a very forceful leavening agent. Buber has received warm testimonial from both friend and foe.[4] Wolf says: "No book about personal relationships has found so widespread an acceptance in current theological writing as Martin Buber's *I and Thou.*" Williams speaks of it as "a book which has rightly exercised on contemporary thought, an influence all

[2] William Barrett, *Irrational Man* (Garden City, N. Y.: Doubleday, 1958), p. 15. For a statement on the impact of Buber beyond philosophy and theology, see Maurice S. Friedman, *Martin Buber* (Chicago: University of Chicago, 1955), pp. vii, 5.

[3] *Martin Buber and Christianity*, tr. by Alexander Dru (New York: Macmillan, 1961), p. 32.

[4] The statements about Buber in this paragraph are from the following sources: William J. Wolf, *Man's Knowledge of God*, (Garden City, N. Y.: Doubleday, 1955), p. 82; Daniel Day Williams, *God's Grace and Man's Hope* (New York: Harper & Row, 1949), pp. 94-95; Lou H. Silberman, "The Search for Relevance," in *A People and its Faith*, ed. by Albert Rose (Toronto: University of Toronto Press, 1959), p. 138; Earl A. Loomis, *The Self in Pilgrimage* (New York: Harper & Row, 1960), p. 64.

out of proportion to its length," and he attributes the power of this book to the fact that "it hits straight at the primary need of our society." Silberman calls attention to Buber's concern "to hold up before man's eyes the true nature of his existence," and to the relevance of his I-It and I-Thou categories "to the whole sweep of man's life." Loomis comments that Buber's contribution was "to establish the theological validity of a psychological principle," viz. that "self-concern does not provide self-fulfillment. We become real, full selves only when we relate to others." Imaginative, vigorous, penterating—yes, Buber's is a voice crying in the wilderness in this age of the mass mind, and those who are sensitive cannot turn a deaf ear to it.

Neither the terminology nor the concept were original, but Buber's imaginative and forceful emphases were, and it is largely due to his genius of expression that they entered so thoroughly into current thought. Even the use of the very terms "It" and "Thou" to express the concept of relation can be found in earlier writers. Buber mentions such usage in von Humboldt and Feuerbach.[5] He further says that although Feuerbach did not elaborate the concept, he gave him a "decisive impetus" in his youth.[6] He was also highly influenced by the developed form of the concept in the neo-Kantian Hermann Cohen [7] of Marburg, who was replaced at his death by Buber as "the representative figure of Western European Jewry." [8] And the concept itself is far from being new to human thought. That God is a "Thou" rather than an

---

[5] Martin Buber, *Between Man and Man,* tr. by Ronald Gregor Smith (New York: Macmillan, 1947), p. 27. Note: *Between Man and Man* is a collection of five essays "filling out and applying" what was said in the shorter work *I and Thou* "with particular regard to the needs of our time."

[6] Martin Buber, *Between Man and Man,* pp. 147-48.

[7] Hermann Cohen, *Religion der Vernunft aus den Quellen des Judentums* (Frankfurt am Main: J. Kauffmann, 1929), pp. 17-18, 22-23, 192-93, 208.

[8] Friedman, *Martin Buber,* p. 258.

24

"It" is basic to all who believe in a personal God. This notion, however, has never been considered as important (either to defend or attack) as it is today and has sometimes been considered "little more than a linguistic convention." [9] Moreover, Jewett, in his treatment of Brunner's concept of revelation, affords a theoretical, as well as chronological, primacy to Ebner's, rather than Buber's, personalism.[10] The I-Thou concept, like all our concepts, is the gift of a long heritage, but it was under the aegis of Martin Buber, a Jewish existentialist, that it gained great popularity and was elevated to the status of intellectual currency.

The Twofold World of I-It and I-Thou

According to Buber the self never exists in isolation but always either in relation (*Verhältnis*), I-Thou, or in connection *(Beziehung)*, I-It. Both I-It and I-Thou are inseparable combinations. They are "primary words" which designate the basic dichotomy in the world and in man's attitude.[11] The "I" that is connected to an "It" is radically different from the "I" that is in relation to a "Thou."

The I-It connection is the most common experience of man in the contemporary Western world, with his near reverence for scientific method. We know about an "It" through the process of reason. Certain identifiable and measurable characteristics are abstracted. For example, we know about a table as something standing thirty inches high, having a rectangular shape, a brown color, and a smooth surface. We can know about other people in the same way. For example, the person

[9] John Hick, *Faith and Knowledge* (Ithaca, N. Y.: Cornell University Press, 1957), pp. 172-73.

[10] Paul King Jewett, *Emil Brunner's Concept of Revelation* (London: James Clarke, 1954), pp. 14, 63 ff.

[11] Buber, *I and Thou*, pp. 3, 31. For a brief summary in Buber's own words, see pp. 33-34.

before us is five feet, ten inches tall, has a muscular frame but is slightly overweight, has blond hair and a light complexion, is in his early thirties, and of Scandinavian extraction. We understand the person as a thing or as an "It," because we abstract these qualities from the person who manifests them. It is quite possible to understand even his behavior in this way. He was deprived of affection by his mother, and therefore he suffers from an inferiority complex. Because of this he is quite servile to his superiors but quite demanding of his inferiors. He also suffers from guilt feelings and thus has a complusion for scrupulous honesty, even in trivial matters. Such a description grows out of an understanding of a person's behavior as a mechanical product of certain experiences, drives, and so on, all quite observable to the careful investigator. The "I" who knows about an "It" has the standpoint of a detached spectator. He understands in terms of generalities and universals. The "It" is an object which can be observed and analyzed, and even another person can be "thingified" in this sense.

The I-Thou relation is much more vivid and intense. The "other" confronts me as a person, in all the richness and mystery of his particular existence. The I-Thou relationship is reciprocal. I am no longer a detached spectator observing a static object; I am now personally involved with another person who is dynamic and free and who is constantly in the process of becoming. I encounter him in his wholeness and concreteness. I see him as he stands in direct relationship to me; I do not grasp him, but he presents himself to me. For example, I do not see merely someone who is compelled by certain drives and impulses, but a free person who makes his own decisions. I am grasped by the fact that he, too, experiences anxiety, despair, guilt, and the threat of death, and that he is a person not a mechanism. He resists any effort to thingify him and to confine him as an object of nature within

26

the phenomenal world. I do not come to know the other, in this personal sense, by discursive means but by "letting myself go" so that the other may break through to me. If I am hostile, or even tired, and therefore uninterested, I will keep the other person at a distance and he will not become a "Thou" for me. I must be fully and completely open to him. There is a feeling of rapport between the two persons. Quite different from the knowledge we had about him is the immediate knowledge of the other person in our presence. To encounter another person is to enter into a profound and a deeply moving relationship.

An illustration may prove helpful in evoking an appreciation of the I-Thou relation. Let us consider the case of a woman who, as a member of an organization, receives the duty of delivering a charity basket of food and clothing. The one who is to be the recipient is known as a name, as the group's "project," as a charity case, as a dweller in a certain slum district, and so on. In the course of delivering the charity basket, there is an opportunity for two people to visit. They soon find such common areas for discussion as problems involved in bringing up children. All of a sudden the realization bursts upon the visitor that this is a "real live person" with whom she is in contact. A charity case and a slum dweller are no longer adequate descriptions, and "project" seems to be a very inappropriate word. The other is known as a person, and the relationship has shifted radically. It is such vivid, personal, and mysterious occurrences as these which are referred to by the term "I-Thou."

Certain very tempting misunderstandings of Buber's view must be exposed at the outset. Neither the vocalizing of the word "Thou" nor the physical presence of other human beings is sufficient to establish an I-Thou relation. Buber is emphatic: "To utter the sound *Thou* with the vocal organs is by no means the same as saying the uncanny primary word." [12] More-over, he states explicitly that the words "he" or "she" can replace "It" in the combination "I-It" without any change occurring in the primary word.[13] Moreover, that which would commonly be considered a physical object (e.g., a stone or a tree), and not at all personal, may become a "Thou." [14] Buber's I-It/I-Thou dichotomy is far more complex and involved than the grammarian's dichotomies of person and gender.

A second misunderstanding of Buber's view is to describe the I-Thou relation as a development from the basic attitude of I-It. In view of the complexity of the primary word "I-Thou," it might seem to follow that this relation is established only after considerable development, but Buber maintains that I-Thou is chronologically prior in development to I-It. He contends that the child's first efforts are not to perceive objects but to establish relations,[15] and that when this is accomplished, there is "a saying of *Thou* without words." Buber speaks of this effort of the part of infants to establish relation as "the *a priori* of relation, *the inborn Thou.*" He argues that "the thing, like the *I,* is produced late," and consequently he makes the assertion: "In the beginning is relation." I-Thou is not a special human achievement but a basic human situation.[16]

Although Buber is expressing a profound truth, his articulation of it may be unduly oversimplified. The "inborn Thou" does not eliminate the significance of impersonal elements for fostering personal relationships. Daniel Day Williams

[12] *Ibid.,* p. 34. For a full discussion distinguishing between genuine and pseudo relations see Buber, *Between Man and Man,* pp. 19 ff.

[13] Buber, *I and Thou,* p. 3.

[14] *Ibid.,* p. 23; *Between Man and Man,* p. 10.

[15] For experiments and case studies supporting such a view see Jean Piaget, *The Construction of Reality in the Child,* tr. by Margaret Cook (New York: Basic Books, 1954), which is a study of the development of the concepts of objects, space, causality, and time.

[16] Buber, *I and Thou,* p. 27.

cites, as examples, impersonal factors in laws, in institutions, and in rational ethical principles, and insists that they "enter into and support the growth of the personal factors." He insists that "factors of consciousness and mentality and moral freedom" do not exhaust the wonder of human personality, for the great wonder is that these factors arise and operate within an impersonal framework.[17] Gibson Winter contends that the church's mission of renewing life is hampered if life is not ministered to in its wholeness. He feels that Buber's separation of I-Thou from the "alien ground" of I-It reflects a deep split in contemporary society, and that we should not perpetuate this dichotomy but minister to the wholeness of life.[18] Buber is quite aware of the *necessity* of the I-It attitude (a point which his critics are sometimes prone to overlook), but Buber does seem to ignore or at least to minimize its possibilities for positive contribution to I-Thou relations.

It is just such a minimization of the significance of I-It elements in human relations that prepares Buber to think of the divine-human encounter as completely devoid of I-It elements. My major contention is that the elimination of I-It elements from divine-human encounter is neither justifiable nor desirable. While I am in basic agreement with the thrust of Buber's position, I would modify his understanding of the encounter between persons by assigning a more creative role to impersonal elements involved in it. It is this difference in understanding the human I-Thou relation that produces the divergence in the understanding of how revelation yields doctrine that will be advanced later in this book.

Despite this oversimplification of Buber's articulation of the I-Thou relation, he elaborates this important distinction in a very creative and forceful manner. As was indicated in

[17] *God's Grace and Man's Hope*, p. 97. Cf. p. 36.
[18] *The Suburban Captivity of the Churches* (New York: Macmillan, 1962), p. 186.

the introduction to this chapter, it is the simplicity of Buber's thought that gives it both force and penetration. Even so, when we have glimpsed that to which he points us, we may need to add qualifications if that perspective which gave such original illumination is to continue to be satisfactory.

One example of the force and penetration which Brunner achieves with his emphasis upon I-Thou relation is seen in his creative option to the contemporary alternatives of individualism and collectivism, both of which are strongly opposed by Buber.

Individualism understands only a part of man, collectivism understands man only as a part: neither advances to the wholeness of man, to man as a whole. Individualism sees man only in relation to himself, but collectivism does not see *man* at all it sees only "society." With the former man's face is distorted, with the latter it is masked.[19]

Both are human attempts to escape solitude; individualism by glorifying it, and collectivism by overpowering and numbing it.

Buber calls for relation not between man and himself, nor between man and the collective mass or aggregate, but between man and man. He insists that we must break through our solitude to attain a transforming meeting with the other. And he distinguishes between "community," which is a being *"with* one another of a multitude of persons," and "collectivism," which is "not a binding but a bundling together" of individuals.[20]

Genuine relation can obtain only between genuine persons. Buber speaks bitingly of the choice between individualism and collectivism as "the false alternative with which the thought

[19] Buber, *Between Man and Man,* p. 200.
[20] *Ibid.,* p. 31. Cf. pp. 64, 80.

of our epoch is shot through." He contends that both the individual and the aggregate are abstractions and that neither is the fundamental fact of existence, which is rather to be found in man with man. Buber says: "I call this sphere, which is established with the existence of man as man but which is conceptually still uncomprehended, the sphere of 'between'" (das Zwischenmenschliche). To help us further comprehend this sphere Buber says: "On the far side of the subjective, on this side of the objective, on the narrow ridge, where *I* and *Thou* meet, there is the realm of 'between.'" Moreover, he insists that "'between' is not an auxiliary construction, but the real place and bearer of what happens between men." Neither a single one, nor the sum total of all the people in a group, is basic but the relation between persons. Buber is convinced that starting with the concept of betweenness makes possible a more adequate understanding of both the single component and the aggregate of a group of people. Buber eschews both individualism and collectivism and goes between the horns of the dilemma to something that is not a compromise but quite new and startling.[21]

Buber's concept of reality as betweenness has an interesting parallel in contemporary physics, which sees reality not in matter but in the forces of energy between what we experience as matter. We have no perception of these forces, but the matter that we do perceive is really nothing more than a polarization of the forces that are the basic, but imperceptible, realities of our universe.

The "I" of man, like the world in which he lives, is twofold, for the "I" of the I-It is different from the "I" of I-Thou. However, Buber is quite clear that each human being includes both kinds of "I."

There are not two kinds of man, but two poles of humanity.

[21] *Ibid.*, pp. 202-5.

"No man is pure person and no man pure individuality. None is wholly real, and none wholly unreal. Every man lives in the twofold *I*." [22] Whether a man is a person or an individual is thus a matter of degree not of kind. It is a question of whether person or individuality is predominant, not simply of which one is present. We call a man a person or an individual on the basis of whether he is "defined by person" or "defined by individuality." In one place Buber illustrates this with an interesting figure of speech. He says that it is a question of which "I" is the architect and which his assistant, at any particular moment. But he quickly modifies this by saying that the "I" of I-Thou can never be the assistant, so it is rather a question of whether or not it remains the architect.[23] Buber speaks of the word "I" as "the true shibboleth of mankind." [24] What a man means when he says "I" is the determining factor in whether person or individuality is dominant in him. But while either I-It or I-Thou must be dominant, both are present in all men. We may talk about the two poles of I-It and I-Thou, but we actually live somewhere between them.

God as the Ultimate Thou

The admixture of I-It elements in I-Thou encounter with humans is not, according to Buber, applicable to encounter with God. This raises some vexing questions. How do we encounter a pure Thou without any admixture of I-It elements? And even if we could, how could we know that we have done so? What is a Thou in itself, without any I-It elements? With such questions as these let us proceed to a consideration

[22] Buber, *I and Thou*, p. 65.
[23] Martin Buber, *Eclipse of God* (New York: Harper & Row, 1952), p. 166.
[24] Buber, *I and Thou*, p. 65.

of Buber's development of this position and an evaluation of its tenability.

Up to this point in our exposition of Buber, his I-Thou and I-It concepts may seem somewhat similar to Jean-Paul Sartre's distinction between *pour-soi* and *en-soi*,[25] except for the latter's strong strain of individualism. But we now come to a very prominent contrast growing out of this difference. Whereas Sartre came to the conclusion that there is no God, Buber finds himself led to God as the ultimate "Thou." In this regard Buber comments:

The problem that "torments" the existentialist thinker of our age, insofar as he does not, like Sartre, dismiss it out of hand, lies deeper than Sartre thinks. It focuses finally in the question of whether the perseverance of the "religious need" does not indicate something inherent in human existence. Does existence really mean, as Sartre thinks, existing "for oneself" encapsuled in one's own subjectivity? Or does it not essentially mean standing *over against* the x—not an x for which a certain quantity could be substituted, but rather the X itself, the undefinable and unfathomable? [26]

Joseph Wood Krutch comments that Sartre's mission is to proclaim: "There is no God and I am his prophet." [27] In similar vein John Courtney Murray describes Sartre as a "scholastic" in the sense that he begins with the affirmation that "God is dead" and asks if this faith is livable (intelligible).[28]

Whereas the I-It attitude finds its "highest concentration

<hr />

[25] Jean-Paul Sartre, *L'être et le néant* (Paris: Librairie Gallimard, 1943), pp. 98-102.
[26] Buber, *Eclipse of God*, p. 90.
[27] "Drama," *The Nation*, December 14, 1946, p. 708.
[28] *The Problem of God* (New Haven: Yale University Press, 1964), p. 114. See pp. 119-21 for Murray's discussion of the religious values of post-modern atheism.

and illumination" in philosophical knowledge, the I-Thou attitude finds its "highest intensity and transfiguration" when God becomes a partner in the relation.[29] Buber's philosophy is avowedly and unabashedly theistic, and the theistic element is not peripheral but central.

However, Buber's opposition to individualism is equally ardent with his devotion to theism. Buber criticizes the sublime misunderstanding of God which led Kierkegaard to take up the life of loneliness, especially through the renunciation of Regina Olsen, as a religious act.[30] Other creatures, far from being obstacles, are the very way to God, and "God wants us to come to him by means of the Reginas he has created and not by renunciation of them."

In contrast with Kierkegaard, Buber considers relation with God and community with fellowmen, including the political community, quite compatible.[31] However, the "so-called" collective decisions are a continual threat to personal responsibility and personal decision. To join a political group and

[29] Buber, *Eclipse of God,* p. 61.

[30] Buber, *Between Man and Man,* pp. 50-58. Compare Buber's criticism of Kierkegaard with Bonhoeffer's letter of December 18, 1943. "I am sure we ought to love God in our *lives* and in all the blessings he sends us. We should trust him in our lives, so that when our time comes, but not before, we may go to him in love and trust and joy. But, speaking frankly, to long for the transcendent when you are in your wife's arms is, to put it mildly, a lack of taste, and it is certainly not what God expects of us. We ought to find God and love him in the blessings he sends us. If he pleases to grant us some overwhelming earthly bliss, we ought not to try and be more religious than God himself. For then we should spoil that bliss by our presumption and arrogance; we should be letting our religious fantasies run riot and refusing to be satisfied with what he gives. Once a man has found God in his earthly bliss and has thanked him for it, there will be plenty of opportunities for him to remind himself that these earthly pleasures are only transitory, and that it is good for him to accustom himself to the idea of eternity, and there will be many hours in which he can say with all sincerity, 'I would that I were home'" (Dietrich Bonhoeffer, *Letters and Papers from Prison,* ed. by Eberhard Bethge, tr. by Reginald H. Fuller [New York: Macmillan, 1953], p. 113).

[31] Buber, *Between Man and Man,* pp. 66-67.

share in "collective" decisions is to surrender political responsibility and to fall from faith. But, in spite of these dangers, if personal responsibility is maintained the life in community and the life in relation are both compatible and beneficial.

Each particular "Thou" implies or involves the eternal "Thou." Sometimes Buber says that through the particular "Thou" we feel the "breath" of the eternal "Thou." At other times he says that in relation to a particular "Thou" we "look out toward the fringe of" the eternal "Thou." Buber also speaks of the particular "Thou" as enabling us to "glimpse through to" the eternal "Thou." Indeed, he does not shy away from saying that in the very act of addressing each "Thou," we address the eternal "Thou." For Buber, each I-Thou event points clearly and unmistakably in the direction of God, the eternal "Thou." [32]

The I-Thou attitude is not fulfilled until man and God confront one another. Man's sense of "Thou" cannot be consummated in any specific I-Thou event, but only in direct relation with the eternal "Thou." Man's sense of "Thou" cannot be "satiated till he finds the endless *Thou.*" The I-Thou events not only point in the direction of God; they also find their fulfillment there. [33]

God is the eternal "Thou." He cannot, by nature, become an "It," even though man, by nature, is compelled to think of him in this way. When God is spoken of as "He" rather than "Thou," a metaphor is employed. Other "Thous" may and will become "its," but God is eternally "Thou." [34]

Relationship with God is all-encompassing. This relation gathers up everything and leaves nothing isolated. This does not mean disregard for everything, but rather the seeing of

[32] Buber, *I and Thou,* pp. 6, 63, 75, 101.
[33] *Ibid.,* pp. 75, 80.
[34] *Ibid.,* pp. 100, 112.

everything encompassed in the one, supreme "Thou."[35] "God is not an object beside objects and hence cannot be reached by renunciation of objects. God, indeed, is not the cosmos, but far less is he Being *minus* cosmos. He is not to be found by subtraction and not to be loved by reduction." [36] Buber is quite emphatic that God is not reached by way of renunciation.

Neither is God found, of course, by the opposite of renunciation. "To look away from the world, or to stare at it, does not help a man to reach God; but he who sees the world in him stands in his presence." The eternal "Thou" encompasses all the spheres in which relation may occur, but is not encompassed in them. The eternal "Thou" completes and unifies all the relations that occur within these spheres, though he is not partial as they are. The eternal "Thou" is the center to which the "extended lines" of relations stretch, and the point at which they meet. When we enter into relation with God, no isolation remains, and we are sharing to the highest possible degree.[37]

The God who is eternally "Thou" is not far off and difficult to confront. We do not find God by seeking for him. We do not elicit God from some "given." God, rather, "is the Being that is directly, most nearly, and lastingly, over against us, that may properly only be addressed, not expressed." [38] And so, God is not far from us. When we are not in an I-Thou relation with God the fault lies with the "I" rather than with the "Thou."

Unless we exercise some care we may easily confuse two widespread views of religious life with Buber's understanding of the relation between man and God. For Buber the reality

[35] *Ibid.*, pp. 78-79. Cf. p. 99.
[36] Buber, *Between Man and Man,* p. 58.
[37] Buber, *I and Thou,* pp. 75, 79, 81, 100-101.
[38] *Ibid.*, pp. 80-81.

of the encounter with the divine is found in the sphere between man and God, not in the feeling which brings God
into man, nor in the mystic merging of man and God.

The I-Thou relation with God is more than a feeling of
dependence upon God. "Feeling" is too restricted a term to
serve as a substitute for the "personal totality" which is
involved in an encounter.[39] The more accurately the element
of feeling is isolated and defined, the more the emphasis is
unbalanced and the more the character of relation is misunder-
stood. Even though a feeling may be considered "ever so
essential," it is nevertheless "a mere accompaniment to the
relation." [40] "Feeling" is a psychological term and a relative
term, and thus it is not applicable to the metapsychical and
metaphysical (or ontic) fact of absolute relation. "The dialogical situation can be adequately grasped only in an ontological
way. But it is not to be grasped on the basis of the ontic
of personal existence, or of that of two personal existences,
but of that which has its being between them, and transcends
both." [41] Feeling is not a relation between men but an emotion within man. Man cannot be understood purely in terms
of what is within him, apart from a consideration of the
relations which are possible for him.[42] To understand the
religious situation as consisting essentially of man's feeling
of dependence on God is to empty one of the bearers of
relation, and hence to destroy the reality of the relation.[43]

It may be objected that since the feeling is one of *dependence,*
both partners of the relation are sustained. But the feeling,

[39] Martin Buber, *Two Types of Faith,* tr. by Norman P. Goldhawk (New
York: Macmillan, 1952), p. 8.

[40] Buber, *I and Thou,* p. 81. Cf. Emil Brunner, *Man in Revolt,* tr. by
Olive Wyon (Philadelphia: Westminster, 1947), p. 252. For a more detailed,
and more extreme, critique of theology based on feeling, see Brunner's *Die
Mystik und das Wort.*

[41] Buber, *Between Man and Man,* p. 204.

[42] *Ibid.,* p. 199.

[43] Buber, *I and Thou,* p. 83.

even though it be one of dependence on God, is still entirely within man. To illustrate this let us consider Schleiermacher, certainly one of the foremost, if not the chief, spokesmen of the view of religion as the feeling of dependence on God. Schleiermacher contends that piety or religious feeling, along with knowledge and morality, has "a province of its own *in the mind* . . . in which it has unlimited sway." [44] In order to make the current term "feeling" more precise and scientifically useful, Schleiermacher excludes from its meaning anything that is not immediate self-consciousness.[45] And so, Buber is quite justified in his claim that the feeling of dependence is within man rather than between man and God.

Buber also distinguishes his mature position from mysticism, a view he once held. He states that the mystical phase was a stage he "had to pass through" before he "could enter into an independent relationship with being." [46] He relates an incident which was highly influential in his disillusionment with mystical religious experience. Indeed, Arthur A. Cohen dates Buber's change in view from this experience.[47] Buber calls the incident both "an everyday event" and "an event of judgment." After a period of " 'religious' enthusiasm," Buber received an unknown visitor, and although Buber was

[44] F. D. E. Schleiermacher, *On Religion: Speeches to its Cultured Despisers*, tr. by John Oman, abridged by E. Graham Waring (New York: Frederick Ungar, 1955), pp. 17-18. Italics mine.

[45] F. D. E. Schleiermacher, *The Christian Faith*, tr. of the second German edition, ed. by H. R. Mackintosh and J. S. Stewart (New York: Scribner's, 1928), p. 6.

[46] Martin Buber, *Pointing the Way*, tr. and ed. by Maurice Friedman (New York: Harper & Row, 1957), p. ix. For a full discussion of the development of Buber's thought from mysticism to his mature dialogical philosophy see Friedman, *Martin Buber*, pp. 27-53. Also see Buber, *Pointing the Way*, and note the development away from the language of mysticism and emotional religious experience toward the language of dialogue in the first group of essays under the title "Towards Authentic Existence," pp. 3-60. With one exception the essays in this group were written before 1916 when *I and Thou* was sketched.

[47] *Martin Buber* (New York: Hillary House, 1958), p. 45.

friendly, attentive, and open, he confesses that he carried on the visit "without being there in spirit." Buber wronged his visitor only by default—he did not try to discern the questions which the visitor had in his mind but did not ask. Not long after a friend of the now deceased visitor told Buber of the vital questions which caused the despair of this young man and prompted his visit to Buber, in which Buber failed to provide the affirmation of meaning that the young man needed and expected.[48]

This incident shocked Buber and led him to discover that the lack of relation is a very serious deficiency in the mystical form of religious life. Buber did not, however, eliminate all mystical elements and evaluated the mystical experience as "certainly an exalted form of being untrue, but . . . still being untrue." [49] The mystical experience is essentially the swallowing up of man in God, either through the absorption of the human by the divine or through the entering of the human into the divine.[50] Thus, by emptying one of the bearers of relation, the mystic has destroyed the reality of relation. Buber contends that the undifferentiated unity of mysticism is a loss of dialogue with the concern for others, and that it is communion, not with God but merely with oneself.

Buber replaced his earlier emphasis on mysticism and monism with an emphasis on relation and dialogue. Instead of mystic absorption and union, he draws on the categories of "the primal setting at a distance" *(Urdistanz)* and "entering into relation" *(Beziehung)*. He explains the relation between them in these words: "Distance provides the human situation, rela-

[48] Buber, *Between Man and Man*, pp. 13-14.
[49] Buber, *Pointing the Way*, p. x.
[50] *Ibid.*, p. ix; *I and Thou*, pp. 83-84; *Between Man and Man*, p. 43. R. C. Zaehner says that this warning is paralleled in the Hindu and Muslim traditions by Ramanuja and Junayd. *Hindu and Muslim Mysticism* (New York: Oxford University Press, 1960), chaps. 4, 7; *Matter and Spirit* (New York: Harper & Row, 1963), pp. 113-28.

tion provides man's becoming in that situation." [51] For Buber genuine religious relation exists only when the "I" and the "eternal Thou" are distinct yet in communion, so that both remain addressing and addressed.

Brunner's Encounter Theology

Emil Brunner is one of the major theologians to take the concepts of Buber and work out their implications for Christian theology in a thorough and rigorous manner. Buber was one of the prophets of existentialism. It would probably be too strong to say that Brunner is a disciple of Buber, for Brunner has experienced significant influences from other sources, and his contribution is certainly far more than that of reinforcing and expanding Buberian views. Yet it would not be too strong to say that Buber exercised a formative influence on Brunner's thought. Although many have employed Buber's concepts in the service of Christian theology, Brunner is chosen for this study because he is one of the major voices in contemporary dialectical theology. Paul King Jewett, thinking especially of Ebner and Buber, says: "Though the thought of these personalists has had a general influence on the dialectical school of theology, to Brunner belongs the distinction of having pioneered in working out the implications of this approach for the whole range of theological thinking." [52] With some oversimplification, then, it can be said that Brunner's concern is to utilize Buber's insights within the framework of Christian theology.

There are two major sources for Brunner's doctrine of revelation, although it is basic to his theology and there-

[51] Martin Buber, "Distance and Relation," tr. by Ronald Gregor Smith, *The Hibbert Journal*, January, 1951, p. 108.
[52] *Emil Brunner's Concept of Revelation*, p. 67. Cf. James I. Packer, "Contemporary Views of Revelation," *Christianity Today*, December 8, 1958, p. 16.

fore prominent in all his work. One major source is *Wahrheit als Begegnung,* which Jewett describes as "a small but highly stimulating volume and perhaps the most original of any that he has written." [53] Brunner was never happy with the title of the English edition, *The Divine-Human Encounter,*[54] and a later edition preceded by several supplementary essays has been brought out with a literal translation of the German title, *Truth as Encounter.*[55] The second book in which Brunner focuses his attention upon revelation is *Revelation and Reason,* in which he describes his aim as "the formulation of a Christian and theological doctrine of revelation as a doctrine of believing knowledge." [56]

For Brunner, as for Buber, the nature of revelation is personal encounter. Revelation is not the reception of truths from or about God but an I-Thou encounter with God. It has been remarked that "preoccupation with the dimension of the personal" is central "in all of Professor Brunner's writing." [57] This preoccupation is especially evident when Brunner is writing on the doctrine of revelation. He refers to "this two-sided but unambiguous relation, this state of the dependent-independent creature—to be face to face with God according to His will," by the term "personal correspondence." This phrase is an equivalent of Buber's concept of "relation," and is Brunner's main inheritance from Buber. Brunner considers personal correspondence to be "the fundamental category of the Bible," and even affirms that everything the Bible says "is said within this basic structure." And from this he argues that "everything that theology avers

[53] *Emil Brunner's Concept of Revelation,* p. 68.

[54] Tr. by Amandus W. Loos (Philadelphia: Westminster, 1943).

[55] Tr. by Amandus W. Loos and David Cairns (Philadelphia: Westminster, 1964).

[56] Tr. by Olive Wyon (Philadelphia: Westminster, 1946), p. 12.

[57] Amandus W. Loos, "The Translator's Preface," *The Divine-Human Encounter,* p. 5.

must remain within this basic structure and everything that contradicts this fundamental presupposition must be rejected and fought against as an unbiblical and even anti-biblical error of speculation or doctrinal distortion." [58] The notion of personal correspondence or encounter is the *grundmotiv* of Brunner's thought. Jewett remarks that personal correspondence is "the fundamental category in Brunner's concept of revelation." [59] One might even venture to say that for Brunner the doctrine of revelation is the fountainhead of the personal dimension, and that by means of the doctrine of revelation the personal dimension is introduced into the other aspects of his thinking and writing.

Some critics of Brunner feel that the concept of personal correspondence, however dynamic it may be, involves one in subjectivism. For example, Jewett contends that Brunner tells us that faith is a "venture" but gives us no way of determining whether we are venturing in the right or wrong direction.[60] Again, E. C. Homrighausen recognizes personal correspondence as "essential Christianity" but insists that it is not solely sufficient. He uses this illustration: Personal correspondence

is like the motor in an automobile; it is *not* the *body,* and it is quite incapable of functioning without a body. But neither is the automobile body the motor. The motor is the active energy. It must have a body, instruments of control and direction, and it must reckon with the highway. For many . . . the one major question will be: Is God's revelation only like a motor, or does it also include the essentials of a body? And in reply, let those who emphasize the motor, and those who emphasize the body, be wary of a dogmatic answer! [61]

[58] Brunner, *Truth as Encounter,* p. 102.
[59] *Emil Brunner's Concept of Revelation,* pp. 174-75.
[60] *Ibid.,* p. 185.
[61] "The Divine-Human Encounter," *Theology Today,* April, 1944, p. 137.

Such criticisms fail to appreciate fully Brunner's insistence that he is speaking strictly within the context of the Christian community and tradition, and that he is presenting his concept of "truth as encounter" in opposition to both objectivism and subjectivism.[62] And yet I feel sympathetic with the concern, at least, which prompts such criticisms. By excluding propositional elements from the encounter he does subordinate thematic factors to dynamic. If, as is contended in Chapter 7, I-It elements are included in encounter, then both dynamic and thematic factors are included within encounter as the *grundmotiv*.

As is true of most religious reformers, Brunner does not feel that he is advocating something new, but rather that he is promoting a return to pristine Christianity. The personal character of revelation was lost early, but it was there originally. The "It-form" was soon predominant, but the "Thou-form" retains its chronological priority, no matter how long the "It-form" has held and may continue to hold sway. Brunner contrasts the biblical view, with its strong personal element, and "the catechetical homiletical traffic in dogma that is determined by the Greek concept of truth." [63] But it is not a mere pedantic interest in history which has motivated Brunner to become the prophet and champion of "truth as encounter" against "truth as idea." Brunner is convinced that the transition from "Thou-form" to "It-form" was a "transition from one dimension to another." [64] Being convinced that the church could ill afford to lose the personal dimension, Brunner is ex-

[62] In the newly added introduction to *Truth as Encounter,* Brunner describes his theology as being beyond the objectivism of Barth and the subjectivism of Bultmann (pp. 41-50). For a similar discussion opening up to include a wide range of comparison see Emil Brunner, *The Christian Doctrine of the Church, Faith, and the Consummation,* tr. by David Cairns (Philadelphia: Westminster, 1962), pp. 212-25.

[63] Brunner, *Truth as Encounter,* p. 179.

[64] Brunner, *Revelation and Reason,* p. 149.

erting his effort and influence toward effecting a retransition. The personal dimension might be characterized as old in inception but new in recognition and appreciation.

For Brunner the content of revelation is not truths but God. The content of revelation is not *something*—not something about, nor even from God—but *someone,* viz. God himself.[65] Brunner's personalization of revelation is a thoroughgoing endeavor, reaching even to the very content of revelation. But even if the content of revelation is God himself, must we add, with Brunner, that the content of revelation does not include something about God? The "Thou" that we experience in an encounter with God is never an amorphous "Thou." Encounter with God involves both conceptual thought and faith, for he always reveals himself as the "God, who . . ." Thus James Harry Cotton insists: "Revelation as personal encounter—that does not settle the question of doctrine. It aggravates it." [66] To say that revelation is encounter neither answers nor evades the question: "Who is it that we encounter?" This can only be answered by statements in I-It form. In chapter 7 the contention will be developed that such interpretation is an essential aspect of encounter and does not originate solely from subsequent reflection upon encounter.

Brunner sees the personal quality of Christian revelation as one of its major distinctive features. In all religions "revelation" refers to the sudden and unexpected disclosure of a mystery which not only increases man's knowledge but also has significance for his life, whether for good or ill. However, in biblical revelation these characteristics are given "a completely new meaning" because "they are provided with a double signature"—absoluteness and personal character.[67]

With the New Testament we have "a new form of revela-

[65] *Ibid.,* p. 25.
[66] *Christian Knowledge of God* (New York: Macmillan, 1951), p. 143.
[67] Brunner, *Revelation and Reason,* pp. 22-23. Cf. p. 44.

tion" which fulfills the promise of the Old Testament. Jesus Christ (not just words or speech) is himself "the actual content" of the new revelation. God "speaks" with us in Jesus Christ, but "God's way of 'speaking' has changed from the literal 'speaking' (through the Prophets); it has become a more figurative way of 'speaking.' " [68]

Brunner claims that John presents this new revelation in his Prologue "as a theme expressed as the transition from the Word to the Person." In saying that "the Word became flesh," John is not suggesting an hypostatization of the Word, but quite the contrary, that such an hypostatization is no longer possible. The basic theme is: "Behold! more than the 'Word' is here—God Himself is here!" [69]

The relation between man and God is merely approximated on the purely human level, and then only when there is mutual self-disclosure and self-surrender. In such a relationship the other person "ceases to be for me a 'someone-something' and becomes a 'Thou,' " and personal correspondence is established. The difference between the connection with another human being as an object and the relation as a "Thou" is "relative, not absolute; the line of demarcation is not sharp—rather, the actual experience always has a mixed character." Consequently, the relation of personal correspondence between human beings can only be analogous to the unconditional relation between a human being and the divine "Thou." In other words, the I-Thou relation between man and God is absolute, unlike the relative I-Thou relation between two human beings. [70]

Revelation is not an object for persons but an event or process which involves persons. It happens to them and in them. Revelation "presupposes a receptive spiritual subject." [71]

[68] Emil Brunner, *The Christian Doctrine of God,* tr. by Olive Wyon (Philadelphia: Westminster, 1950), pp. 23, 27.
[69] *Ibid.,* p. 24. See his paraphrase of the Johannine Prologue.
[70] Brunner, *Truth as Encounter,* pp. 114-15.
[71] Brunner, *Revelation and Reason,* p. 416.

Revelation occurs when "the 'Thou'-word of God addressed to the soul" evokes a "confession of faith in the form of the answering 'Thou.' " [72] The confession evoked by the Word is a free, personal response, as in the Arminian tradition.

The manner in which the Word works is different from all objective-causal, concrete-magical influences. The Word does not overwhelm, it does not coerce, it does not ignore the one "over against it," but it calls, addresses, threatens, and entreats; it "calls forth" or evokes decision.[73]

Revelation is the personal meeting between the human "I" and the divine "Thou."

In the encounter man must respond with his whole person. The revelation of God is not to be thought of "merely in terms of the discovery of truth," for "it does not affect one side of the nature alone—as, for instance, that of the intellect—but it seizes the inner core of personality." [74] Brunner remarks that the German word *"Glaube,"* and the same is true of "faith" in English, is extremely liable to misunderstanding because it has come to be understood in intellectualistic terms. The complete or whole response of the person to the self-giving of God is called "obedience-in-trust *(Vertrauensgehorsam), pistis."* [75] The intellectualistic reduction of faith is a dangerous misunderstanding because God's self-revelation is not given simply to enlighten our intellect but to evoke the total response of faith as "obedience-in-trust." Not only is the revelation itself personal, but the relation through which it is accomplished is also personal. Thus, it is not adequate to say merely that man hears God's revelation, or believes it (i.e.,

[72] Brunner, *The Christian Doctrine of God,* p. 38.
[73] Brunner, *Revelation and Reason,* p. 416.
[74] Emil Brunner, *The Mediator,* tr. by Olive Wyon (Philadelphia: Westminster, 1947), p. 203.
[75] Brunner, *Truth as Encounter,* p. 104.

with his mind). There is a much deeper and much more vital relationship between man and God, in which man's concern is "to come to *Him,* to trust Him, to be united to Him, to surrender to Him." [76] Faith, in the final analysis, is marked by attitudes of trust, obedience, and love, rather than by doctrines which are merely objects of thought.[77] Brunner has thoroughly personalized revelation, both in scope and in depth.

Brunner remarks that Peter, who was the first to confess Jesus as the Christ, did so "in the dimension of personal encounter," and Brunner further insists that every true believer makes his confession in the "Thou-I" dimension, rather than by a doctrinal statement in the "he-you" dimension.[78] We are reminded of Buber's assertion that a metaphor is employed when God is spoken of as "He" rather than "Thou." [79] Jewett protests Brunner's understanding of Peter's confession: "It is a trifle difficult . . . to see why such stupendous significance should be attached to the difference between the proposition '*Thou* art the Christ' (faith) and the proposition '*He* is the Christ' (witness)." He urges that both statements—confession and witness to it—"are propositions cast in the form of human words and subject to the laws of coherent speech." [80] The difference between faith and witness seems to be basically little more than the direction of address. However, Buber and Brunner have brought to our attention that this is much more than a mere formal distinction. But this difference, important though it is, does not alter the fact that both "Thou art the Christ" and "He is the Christ" have the same referent. Therefore the difference is intensional (connotative), not extensional (denotative). For Brunner, "Thou art the Christ" implies en-

---

[76] Brunner, *The Christian Doctrine of God,* p. 26.
[77] Brunner, *Truth as Encounter,* p. 134. Cf. *The Mediator,* p. 203.
[78] Brunner, *The Christian Doctrine of God,* p. 38.
[79] Buber, *I and Thou,* p. 112.
[80] Jewett, *Emil Brunner's Concept of Revelation,* p. 161.

counter with God in Christ; "He is the Christ" implies more abstract, intellectual knowledge.

Faulty Use of the Analogy of Encounter

Both Buber and Brunner have used the analogy of encounter as the most adequate analogy for speaking of God, and they have said that divine-human encounter is distinguished from human encounter by virtue of being completely free of I-It elements. But can there be an encounter with God without any admixture of I-It? In order to consider this question we must consider the nature of analogy in general and the analogy of encounter in particular. An understanding of the general nature of analogy will help us to see why Buber and Brunner feel compelled to maintain a sharp dichotomy between I-It and I-Thou knowledge of God.

Analogy is a mode of communication which employs a familiar item of experience to point to an unfamiliar item of experience.[81] It proceeds by pointing out a basis of similarity between the two, and also a way of modifying the familiar use of the term. The analogical use of a term is distinguished from the univocal and equivocal use. A term is used univocally when it has the same designation, e.g., "dog" refers univocally to a Collie and an Eskimo Spitz. A term is used equivocally when there is no way of modifying the experience, e.g., "dog" refers equivocally to a canine and to the Dog Star, Sirius. A term is used analogically when there is both a comparison and difference, e.g., "dog" refers analogically to a canine and to a worthless, wretched person. In this example there is an assertion of both similarity and difference at the same time. A person is said to be like a dog (basis of the

[81] For an excellent discussion of analogy from the neo-Thomist point of view see E. L. Mascall, *Existence and Analogy,* (London: Longmans, Green, 1949), chap. 5. For fuller application of this concept to theological discourse see E. L. Mascall, *Words and Images* (New York: Ronald, 1957).

analogy), but only in respect to status or condition (modification of the use of the term). Both the basis of comparison and its limitation are essential to the use of analogy.

How do we speak of God? God cannot be known in the same way in which we know objects in the world. God never confronts us directly, like a physical object. We know God only as he reveals himself to us, and this manifestation comes to us out of the mystery of God's inwardness and freedom. Further, we are not able to confine God within our categories of thought, for they cannot contain the one who is the ground of everything that exists. God transcends all categories of human thought which are bound to the realm of finitude and contingency. Moreover, we cannot employ generalizations in our understanding of God, for he is one and unique and not a member of a class. Because God is pure subject, wholly other, and unique, all human affirmations concerning God are inadequate to express the nature of that to which they refer. Moreover, not only is God essentially beyond the capacity of human language, but further, man's efforts to talk about God are subject to the influence of sin. In a state of alienation and rebellion man disrupts the personal relation that should unite him with God. The disruption of man's relation with the ground of being distorts every facet and dimension of human existence, and man's knowledge of God is among those things which are most influenced by this distortion. In summary, God is necessarily mysterious and unfathomable because of his personality, transcendence, and uniqueness; and furthermore, this mysteriousness and unfathomableness is deepened by man's alienation and estrangement from God.

Consequently, when we speak about God we must employ analogy, unless we confine ourselves to saying what God is not, as in Plotinus' discussion of the ineffable One, or in the Hindu description of Brahman as "not this, not this." Literal or univocal language, however, is impossible because we are forced to talk about the infinite and suprasensible God in terms that have been developed for talking about finite and sensible phenomena. The differences between our knowledge of the phenomenal world and our knowledge of God are such that we cannot speak of the latter simply as if it were a special case of the former. Equivocal language would be of no value, since it uses the same term but gives no suggestion as to how it is to be used in the new context. Since God does not confront us directly, there is nothing to which we can point as the designation of our term. As Farrer says: "About that which is simply unique there can be no discourse." [82] For speaking of God univocal language is not available, and equivocal language is not helpful. We must use analogical language to speak positively about God. However difficult it may be to delineate the limitations of theological analogy, to do so is an essential task. Theological language does not refer to objective matters of fact which can be expressed adequately in rational and factual categories. Every theological affirmation about the transcendent must involve a denial of its literal application and an effort to clarify the meaning which is suggested.

Buber and Brunner employ "encounter" as the best analogy for speaking of our knowledge of God. We know God, not in the manner in which we know objects (I-It and I-he connections) but in the manner in which we know persons (I-Thou relations). Yet the term "encounter" does not apply literally and univocally when we speak of encountering God. How can we modify the use of the term so that it will point from a basic similarity toward the differentiation of our relation with God from encounter with men? The distinction made by Buber and Brunner is that, unlike encounter between persons, the divine-human encounter is completely free of I-It elements. While there is an admixture of I-Thou and I-It in any en-

[82] Austin M. Farrer, *Finite and Infinite* (London: Dacre Press, 1943), p. 23.

counter between persons, the divine-human relation is encounter with a pure Thou and is completely free of I-It elements. This is why encounter theologians insist that knowledge about God is not necessary to encounter with God. If Buber and Brunner were to concede an admixture of I-It in divine-human encounter, then they would have surrendered the means of modifying the understanding of encounter between men so as to allow it to point toward divine-human encounter.

Hepburn attacks the assumption that I-Thou encounters with God are completely free of I-It elements, which are always present to some degree in human encounters.[83] He begins by denying that it is possible to establish a scale of impurity-purity in encounters so that the direction toward the completely pure encounter with God could be indicated. Then he proceeds to illustrate that even when knowledge about the person encountered is largely unconscious, it is nonetheless essential to the encounter. To know the other person as he knows himself, apart from any I-It knowledge about the person to mediate this knowledge to me, would be not to *encounter* the other person but to *become* the other person, in the sense of temporarily assuming his personality. Or, if this is saying too much, it would still be not an *encounter* of another person but a personal experience of one's own. To illustrate Hepburn distinguishes between encountering an angry John and becoming angry oneself. To eliminate I-It elements would not purify but dissolve encounter. Although we do not concur with Hepburn's outright rejection of the analogy of encounter, we are in accord with his conclusion that while Buber and Brunner do give some familiar item of experience as a basis for analogy, they fail in their effort to modify this item of experience. Unless it can be successfully emended, encounter theology lacks an adequate analogy of our relation with God.

[83] Ronald Hepburn, *Christianity and Paradox* (New York: Humanities, 1958), pp. 31-39.

3. Buber's Concept of Revelation

If Buber and Brunner make faulty use of the analogy of encounter, then the concept of revelation that issues from it should also be subject to challenge. In this chapter our aim is to examine the concept of nonpropositional revelation that is set forth in Buber and in the next chapter to examine that of Brunner.

Buber's concept of revelation has greatly influenced contemporary formulations of this doctrine. In one place Buber makes the modest claim: " 'Faith' is not a feeling in the soul of man but an entrance into reality, an entrance into the *whole* reality without reduction and curtailment. This thesis is simple but it contradicts the usual way of thinking." [1] Buber has most assuredly contradicted the usual way of thinking, but he has done so in such a thorough and forceful manner that the way of thinking has changed. Our first task in this chapter is to describe Buber's understanding of the contrast between I-Thou and I-It.

[1] Buber, *Eclipse of God,* p. 11.

BUBER'S CONCEPT OF REVELATION

The Contrast Between Persons and Objects

Buber draws a sharp contrast between objects and persons. We need to explore this contrast because it is the foundation of Buber's concept of revelation. I-It is an objective experience; I-Thou, a personal situation. In other words, in the I-It attitude we are connected to objects; and in the I-Thou attitude, related to persons. Objects ("Its") may be measured and defined; persons ("thous") are free and not static but continually in crises, i.e., making decisions. In I-It, the "I" comes in contact with things or objects. There is no theoretical limit to the number of objects with which one may come in contact, but it is not possible in this attitude to meet other persons as such, for the I-It attitude is not adequate to comprehend another personality. The I-Thou attitude is not a relation to the world without but stirs in the very depth of the person. It is impossible to overstress the personal involvement in the I-Thou attitude. However, we dare not abstract the attitude from the other person who is evoking it. Buber warns: "But guard against wishing to remove it into your soul—for then you annihilate it." [2] Anything, even another human being, can be treated as an object, and in such a case we have adopted the I-It attitude rather than I-Thou. Whether experiences are "inner" or "outer," "secret" or "open," is not the decisive factor.[3] There is a radical difference between the I-It connection with objects and the I-Thou relation to persons.

The I-It world is composed of objects, for that which experiences and uses, just as much as that which is experienced and used, is an object. Whenever the "I" takes on a separate existence from that which is experienced or used, "it also moves, strangely tenuous and reduced to merely functional activity, into the natural, actual event of the separation of the

---

[2] Buber, *I and Thou*, p. 33.
[3] *Ibid.*, p. 5.

body from the world round about it." [4] In this state the "I" becomes self-conscious and considers itself the bearer of perceptions, whose object is the world round about. The it-world consists of bounded or delimited objects, for "it" can exist only when there are other "its" to bind it off or restrict its being. Buber locates the source of man's tendency so to divide the world in "the lust of the human race to whittle away the secret of death." [5] Because there is no vital relation between objects, the primary word "I-It" may be spoken of as "the word of separation." [6]

In the world of I-It the two major activities are experiencing and using. Buber draws this vivid contrast:

> The *I* of the primary word *I-It* makes its appearance as individuality and becomes conscious of itself as subject (of experiencing and using).
> The *I* of the primary word *I-Thou* makes its appearance as person and becomes conscious of itself as subjectivity (without a dependent genitive).[7]

For Buber, experiencing and using are actions that we perform with objects but not with persons. We can only experience and use those things which allow us to be their masters and controllers. By experiencing objects, man continually reconstitutes the world; by using objects, man sustains, relieves, and equips his life.[8] Thus the objects man comes in contact with may be described as "objects of observation, reflection, use, perhaps also of solicitude or help." [9] The world of I-It is the

---

[4] *Ibid.,* p. 23.
[5] *Ibid.,* p. 5.
[6] *Ibid.,* p. 23.
[7] *Ibid.,* p. 62.
[8] *Ibid.,* p. 38.
[9] Buber, *Eclipse of God,* p. 166.

sphere of experiencing and using, and man cannot avoid living in it.

However, there is more to life than experiencing and using. Both I-It and I-Thou attitudes are necessary to "build up human existence." [10] As Buber so aptly puts it: "The life of human beings is not passed in the sphere of transitive verbs alone. It does not exist in virtue of activities alone which have some *thing* for their object." [11] Experiencing and using are necessary functions because they enable us to regulate and preserve life, but it is unfortunate indeed when they crowd out all else, as is so often the case today. Buber cautions: "We only need to fill each moment with experiencing and using, and it ceases to burn." [12] As a matter of fact, it is actually the decrease of man's capacity to enter into relations that is the major factor in the development of the functions of experiencing and using objects.[13]

At times, especially in his earlier work *I and Thou*,[14] Buber is quite sharp in his attacks on the imperializing of the I-It attitude. For example, while readily granting, indeed insisting, that only the it-world can be ordered, he remarks further that this would be "a useless fragment," if we did not "set down the other part of the basic truth . . . namely, a world that is ordered is not the world-order." Again, in like manner, he says: "And in all the seriousness of truth, hear this: without *It* man cannot live. But he who lives with *It* alone is not a man." Further, in the same vein, he remarks: "The aim of self-differentiation is to experience and to use, and the aim of these is 'life,' that is, dying that lasts the span of a man's life." Let us consider one final, and probably the most deroga-

[10] *Ibid.*
[11] Buber, *I and Thou*, p. 4.
[12] *Ibid.*, p. 34.
[13] *Ibid.*, p. 43.
[14] Quotations in this paragraph are from pp. 31, 34, 62-63.

tory, example: "How self-confident is that wisdom which perceives a closed compartment in things, reserved for the initiate and manipulated only with the key. O secrecy without a secret! O accumulation of information! It, always It!" [15] So, while Buber insists that the I-It attitude is necessary to life, he takes no pains to conceal the fact that he considers this attitude quite insufficient of itself for a full human life.

When we enter the I-Thou world, there are no objects, no things, indeed nothing. There is nothing we can master, manipulate, or control. Buber says: "I do not experience the man to whom I say *Thou.* . . . In the act of experience *Thou* is far away." Buber asks the question that is in our minds concerning the I-Thou world, and then answers it.

—What, then, do we experience of *Thou?*
—Just nothing. For we do not experience it. [16]

If we do not experience objects in the I-Thou world, what is the corresponding situation? The corresponding situation is standing in relation to persons.

In the I-It connection man separates the world into individual objects isolated from one another and from himself; but in the I-Thou relation he enters into community with all that confronts him. Buber expresses it succinctly:

Individuality makes its appearance by being differentiated from other individualities.
A person makes his appearance by entering into relation with other persons.
The one is the spiritual form of natural detachment, the other the spiritual form of natural solidarity of connexion. [17]

[15] *Ibid.,* p. 5.
[16] *Ibid.,* pp. 9, 11.
[17] *Ibid.,* p. 62.

The basic distinction here is that we come to know about objects by a process of abstraction, but we come to know persons by being receptive to them in their totality. Note, too, that Buber here uses he term "individual" to refer to one who knows by abstraction, and "person" to refer to one who knows by grasping the other in his wholeness. In the I-It world, the "I" is an individual in the sense of being conscious of itself as a separate entity within a collection of objects; in the I-Thou world, the "I" is a person in the sense of being conscious of itself as sharing its being with other equal persons. Buber says: " 'Know thyself,' means for the person 'know thyself to have being,' for the individual it means 'know thy particular kind of being.' " [18] The person sees himself in relation to other persons; the individual, in arithmetical distinction from other objects.

The primary word I-Thou is thus a word of relation and dialogue. Buber does not, however, mean to imply that the person, because he shares in being, has to surrender in any way his special being, i.e., that which makes him different. Both the individual (I-It) and the person (I-Thou) have their own special being. However, for the person (I-Thou) it is simply there and not "his observation point"; but the individual (I-It) "revels" in it and establishes his own special being as a point of observation from which to experience the world. Indeed, Buber goes on to argue that there is a greater fictional element, i.e., less reality, in the special being of an individual than in that of a person. When a man is mastered by individuality, the "I" sinks more and more deeply into unreality, and the man leads what Buber calls "a hidden subterranean and as it were cancelled existence." On the other hand, the more fully the "I" relates and shares itself, the more real it becomes. Reality is not attained by individuation but by shar-

[18] *Ibid.,* p. 64.

ing and outgoing. In the relation between "I" and "Thou," the "I" can neither be isolated nor surrendered.[19]

However, something is surrendered by one who leaves the world of individuated objects and enters the world of relation. He must surrender "that false self-asserting instinct that makes a man flee to the possessing of things before the unreliable, perilous world of relation which has neither density nor duration and cannot be surveyed." In other words, man must give up his quest for certainty and security. In the I-Thou realm, the person does not *possess* reality but *shares in it,* i.e., it "neither merely belongs to him nor merely lies outside him." We cannot appropriate reality to ourselves, for there can be no reality where there is no sharing, and the greater the sharing, the fuller the reality.[20]

Even so, it is not always necessary that the sharing be recognized by both parties. Buber says quite clearly: "Even if the man to whom I say *Thou* is not aware of it in the midst of his experience, yet relation may exist. For *Thou* is more than *It* realizes." [21] It is possible, then, for another to become a "Thou" for me, even though he himself is in the I-It attitude. This is possible because we are not dealing here in the realm of objects but of personal attitudes. The I-Thou attitude is established when a person has given up all attempts to possess reality as an object and seeks, rather, to share in reality. It is possible to have such an attitude toward another whether or not he has it toward you.

The primary word I-Thou can be spoken only with the whole being, in contrast with the primary word I-It, which can never be spoken with the whole being. When an individual stands in an I-It connection he not only makes an object of, or "thingifies," the man or thing which is his "It," but in so

[19] *Ibid.,* pp. 64-65.
[20] *Ibid.,* p. 78.
[21] *Ibid.,* p. 9.

doing sees it in connection with himself, and to do this must make his self an object among other objects. And so in the I-It connection only a part of the "I" knows about a part of the "It." In the I-Thou relation there is no abstraction from the object of knowledge and no detachment of the subject. When the I-Thou attitude is established the whole person, and not just a portion, is inevitably involved.

In the I-It realm objects are passive recipients of the action of the subject. In other words, the action is solely performed by the subject (I), and solely received by the object (It) which is experienced or used. A major distinction between I-It and I-Thou is that the former is described as passive and the latter as active. In the following description of these two modes of being, these characteristics head the list. "Each thing and being has a twofold nature: the passive, absorbable, usable, dissectible, comparable, combinable, rationalizable, and the other, the active, non-absorbable, unusable, undissectible, incomparable, noncombinable, nonrationalizable." [22] You may take an object and keep it as long as you wish, but it is never able to give itself to you.[23] The I-It attitude involves a monologue in which the agent experiences and uses passive objects.

In the I-Thou realm, the "I" and the "Thou" are not related as subject and object but as partners who have entered into a dialogue. From the fact that relation can be established neither solely by, nor apart from, the person's agency, Buber concludes that "relation means being chosen and choosing, suffering and action in one." [24] Both "I" and "Thou" are active, and both are passive. There is a reciprocal influence in which each element affects and is affected by the other.[25] A "Thou" cannot be mastered. A "Thou" may approach us

[22] Buber, *Pointing the Way,* p. 27.
[23] Buber, *I and Thou,* p. 32.
[24] *Ibid.,* p. 76.
[25] *Ibid.,* p. 15.

when we have not summoned it and may vanish despite our efforts to prolong its presence. An "I" and a "Thou" confront each other on an equal basis. Neither is subject to the manipulation or control of the other, but rather there is a mutual giving and receiving. Each element presents itself to, and is brought out by, the other.[26] And so Buber contends that "all real living is meeting."[27] The I-Thou relation involves a dialogue in which two subjects encounter one another as coequals.

Objects in the I-It connection can be analyzed, understood, known, and communicated to others. The it-world, unlike the thou-world, is set in the framework of space and time. Thus the various components of the it-world may be measured and compared with one another. Such a world is orderly, reliable, public, and relatively stable. Although each individual's actual experience is private, it is experience of objects which are common to all observers, and therefore he can make himself understood by others. The objects of our experience can, if we so desire, become objects of our understanding, for they are subject to our control.[28]

In sharp contrast, that which is confronted in the I-Thou relation is incommunicable. We intuit rather than reason discursively in the I-Thou realm. Genuine faith (encounter)

says something to me, but what it says to me cannot be revealed by any esoteric information; for it has never been said before nor is it composed of sounds that have ever been said. It can neither be interpreted nor translated, I can have it neither explained nor displayed; it is not a *what* at all, it is said into my very life; it is no experience that can be remembered independently of the situation, it remains the address of that moment and cannot be isolated, it remains the question of a questioner and will have its answer.[29]

---

[26] *Ibid.*, pp. 32-33.
[27] *Ibid.*, p. 11.
[28] *Ibid.*, pp. 31-33, 100.
[29] Buber, *Between Man and Man*, p. 12.

At first glance this may seem like a pathetic situation, but this is far from Buber's intention. Buber's emphasis is not on man's quandary in such a situation but on his reception of that which far exceeds the knowledge of objects in the it-world. We grasp at that which is too great to be contained. Buber asks the question that is on our minds, and then answers it:

—What, then, do we know of *Thou?*
—Just everything. For we know nothing isolated about it any more.[30]

The world's comprehensibility is but a "footstool" to its incomprehensibility, which has "a new, a wonderful secret to bestow. . . . The world is not comprehensible, but it is embraceable." [31]

Moreover, we cannot teach people, by means of precepts, how to enter into relations; it can only be indicated.[32] Furthermore, the only way it can be indicated is by way of negation.[33] It is not really a case of teaching but of evoking the proper attitude. In the encounter, the "other" does not lead us to knowledge but to personal confrontation. Emphasis on the impersonal quality of teaching is also found in Brunner. He insists that the best teacher is the one who weans the pupil from any dependence upon himself.[34] Brunner also remarks: "The fact that it was another than myself who led me to the truth is, so far as truth is concerned, an *accident.*" [35] It-truth is impersonal and may be taught; the I-Thou relation is incommunicable.

[30] Buber, *I and Thou,* p. 11.
[31] Buber, *Pointing the Way,* p. 27.
[32] Buber, *I and Thou,* p. 77.
[33] *Ibid.,* p. 78. Note: Buber's expression is "by the drawing of a circle which excludes everything that is not this going out."
[34] Brunner, *Revelation and Reason,* p. 365; *God and Man,* tr. by David Cairns (New York: Macmillan, 1936), p. 47.
[35] Brunner, *Revelation and Reason,* pp. 365-66. Italics mine.

But true as this may be, encounter theology seems to be stopping with a half truth. It should be added that a teacher who can establish an I-Thou relation with his pupils is better enabled to communicate it-truth to them. Also, by providing an atmosphere in which pupils are willing to make a mental risk or venture, he is better able to help them discover truth for themselves. And so, it-truth, impersonal though it be, does not seem to preclude, but indeed to benefit from, an I-Thou relation. It is such a combination of thou-truth and it-truth that would seem to be a preferable description of encounter. But Buber contrasts these sharply, and it is now our task to examine the concept of revelation that Buber develops from a notion of encounter which sharply excludes I-It elements.

Disclosure of the Presence

At the outset let us distinguish between two terms in rabbinic theology—*Gilluy ha-Shekinah* and *Mattan Torah*. These refer to different meanings of the term "revelation." *Gilluy ha-Shekinah* means "the disclosure of the Presence." *Mattan Torah* means "the giving of the Torah." The latter term involves the revelation of a content, and this understanding of revelation is rejected by Buber. It is in this regard that we see Buber standing in sharpest contrast with conservative Jewish theology. In the next section we will see how Buber understands the function of the Torah, and it is here that he stands in sharpest contrast with liberal Jewish theology. The function of the Torah is not to reveal general moral truths but to make possible a special revelation to a particular man at a particular moment.

Before we go on to discuss revelation as "the disclosure of the Presence," let us consider Buber's distinction between the word administered by the priests and the word of which the prophet is the bearer. The former is a verbal form of rite and is offered by man to God; the latter comes from God to man and subdues man. The priests are able to "handle" the Torah without any yearning for God's presence. The prophet, on the other hand, is subject to a word which "suddenly descends into the human situation, unexpected and unwilled by man . . . free and fresh like the lightening." It is a personal word, spoken by a person and to a person, and yet the one who speaks remains "incomprehensible, irregular, surprising, overwhelming, sovereign." The word of revelation, as Buber understands it, is the word that the prophet bears.[36]

Buber rejects the notion that revelation is of propositional content and insists rather that revelation is encounter. Buber says that man "receives not a specific 'content' but a Presence, a Presence as power." This Presence as power includes three elements: (1) absolute mutuality of action and binding in relation; (2) "inexpressible confirmation of meaning" ("nothing can any longer be meaningless"); (3) this meaning pertains to this life and world.[37] Revelation is *Gilluy ha-Shekinah*, the disclosure of the Presence.

For Buber the important thing is not knowledge about God but relation with him. As a matter of fact, knowledge about God is not even considered necessary. "It is not necessary to know something about God in order really to believe in Him: many true believers know how to talk to God but not *about* Him." [38] Moreover, dialogue with God is never a source of information about God.[39] Neither analytical nor synthetic procedures nor reflective investigation of any sort are means by which the meaning of existence may be discovered. The meaning of existence cannot be grasped by the mind alone, but

[36] Martin Buber, *The Prophetic Faith*, tr. by Carlyle Witton-Davies (New York: Macmillan, 1949), p. 164. See also p. 175.
[37] Buber, *I and Thou*, p. 110.
[38] Buber, *Eclipse of God*, p. 40. Cf. *I and Thou*, p. 115.
[39] Buber, *Between Man and Man*, p. 12.

only by the whole being. In Buber's words, it is to be apprehended "in living action and suffering itself, in the unreduced immediacy of the moment." [40]

Although the writer concurs with the general emphasis and development of Buber's thought, it is here that he must express his major dissatisfaction with Buber's formulation. While I agree that knowledge about God is subordinate to relation with him, and that not merely an intellectual response but a total, existential response is necessary to encounter, I cannot concur in the views that knowledge about God is neither necessary to encounter nor involved in it. It is my contention, later to be defended, that knowledge about God is an essential element of divine-human encounter, and that encounter with God includes I-It elements. Another basis of distinguishing between encounter with God and man is suggested, and the nature and significance of a personal, existential knowledge within encounter is discussed. At this point we may simply observe that if encounter involves a total response, it seems arbitrary to consider intellectual assent as unnecessary to and an inevitable distortion of encounter.

To return to our exposition, Buber insists that propositions are not adequate to convey revelation. "Every religious utterance is a vain attempt to do justice to the meaning which has been attained. All religious expression is only an intimation of its attainment." [41] In revelation the mystery of God's personal being has become present for us, and in this relation "we have 'known' it, but we acquire no knowledge from it which might lessen or moderate its mysteriousness." [42] Moreover, even if we were able to describe the meaning of revelation adequately, this would still not be revelation for others,

[40] Buber, *Eclipse of God,* p. 49.
[41] *Ibid.,* p. 50.
[42] Buber, *I and Thou,* p. 111.

for it would only be knowledge about God's word rather than God's word for them.

Buber feels that religion and religious knowledge, on one hand, and philosophy and philosophical knowledge, on the other hand, are in rather sharp contrast. The contrast grows largely out of the difference in the role of thought in the areas of religion and philosophy. In religion thinking is a partial activity; in philosophy it dominates. Buber expresses it this way:

> In religious reality the person has concentrated himself into a whole, for it is only as a unified being that he is able to live religiously. In this wholeness thought is naturally also included as an autonomous province but one which no longer strives to absolutize its autonomy. A totalization also takes place in genuine philosophers but no unification. Instead, thinking overruns and overwhelms all the faculties and provinces of the person. In a great act of philosophizing even the finger-tips think—they no longer feel.[43]

Religion, as Buber understands it, is "essentially the act of holding fast to God," not just to some image or concept of God. Philosophical concepts of God are merely ideas about him. Taking a hint from Pascal, Buber says that the "passion" peculiar to philosophers is pride, and that they offer men their own system rather than the God of Abraham. However, Buber disavows any implications that philosophy is not able to "lead to and contain truth." [44] Nonetheless, religion is not primarily concerned with "thought-relations" but with the relation between "I" and "Thou." [45]

[43] Buber, *Eclipse of God*, pp. 60-61.
[44] *Ibid.*, pp. 60-61, 159, 67, 68, 60.
[45] It is interesting to note, in this connection, that Baillie has argued that the usual philosophical use of the term "revelation" is metaphorical and that the religious use is primary. The gist of his argument is that the statement, "The object of thought reveals itself to me," is not literally but metaphorically true, since it is based on a personification of the object, for only persons, and not objects, can reveal themselves (*The Idea of Revelation in Recent Thought*, pp. 24-25).

The religious situation is characterized by paradox or antinomy. Paradox or antinomy is inevitable. Buber calls it an "essential and indissoluble" element of man's religious situation. He gives this warning to those who would dissolve or minimize the antinomies of religious experience.

He who accepts the thesis and rejects the antithesis does injury to the significance of the situation. He who tries to think out a synthesis destroys the significance of the situation. He who strives to make the antinomy into a relative matter abolishes the significance of the situation. He who wishes to carry through the conflict of the antinomy other than with his life transgresses the significance of the situation. The significance of the situation is that it is lived, and nothing but lived, continually, ever anew, without foresight, without forethought, without prescription, in the totality of its antinomy.[46]

The philosophical antinomy can be resolved in such a way as to reconcile the paradoxical elements, but the elements of the religious antinomy are united only by being lived. Buber understands the function of paradox as that of pointing rather than expressing. In other words, paradox does not contain the truth but points us toward it. Paradox can neither be resolved nor escaped by the religious man, but it can be lived by those who will take their stand before God and take both elements of the antinomy into their lives.[47]

According to Buber, revelation and the recipient of revelation mutually influence one another. Those who understand revelation as the impartation of specific information by God think of the persons to whom revelation comes as passive agents—indeed, the more passive they are, the more pure and genuine is the revelation. For Buber, on the other hand, "the eternal, primal phenomenon, present here and now, of

[46] Buber, *I and Thou*, p. 95.
[47] *Ibid.; Eclipse of God*, pp. 59-60.

that which we term revelation . . . is . . . that a man does not pass, from the moment of the supreme meeting, the same being as he entered into it." Revelation always makes a difference to a man; something always happens to him— "At times it is like a light breath, at times like a wrestling-bout, but always—it *happens*." Above all, when the eternal mystery reveals itself to us, it proclaims itself to us as "salvation." [48] Man, in turn, conditions revelation.

Revelation does not pour itself into the world through him who receives it as through a funnel; it comes to him and seizes his whole elemental being in all its particular nature, and fuses with it. The man, too, who is the "mouth" of the revelation, is indeed this, not a speaking-tube or any kind of instrument, but an organ, which sounds according to its own laws; and to sound means to *modify*.[49]

The idea is not that revelation changes, for it is the same eternal revelation that confronts all men, but that it is conditioned by the human partner of revelation, and so in the act of transmission it becomes modified.

Revelation and the Torah

Buber's insistence that revelation is the disclosure of the Presence and not the giving of the Torah is bound to raise the question: What, then, is the function of the Torah? It is Buber's answer to this question which most clearly distinguishes him from liberal Jewish theology. The Torah does not, for Buber, embody general moral truths. It serves its function strictly within the present by recalling the possibility of relation.

[48] Buber, *I and Thou*, pp. 109-11.
[49] *Ibid.*, p. 117.

Buber distinguishes between two types of faith—*emunah* (faith as trust in a person) and *pistis* (faith as acknowledgment of truth). The essential element of both types of faith is an attitude which does not depend upon reasons, but this may take two basic forms: trust in a person or acknowledgment of truth.[50] The absence of dependence upon reasons constitutes the attitude as one of faith, and the relationship to persons or truths differentiates faith into *emunah* and *pistis*. Religious faith includes these two types, but in this context they are "in the sphere of the unconditioned, that is, the relationship of faith is here no longer one towards a person conditioned in himself or a fact conditioned in itself and only unconditioned for me, but to one which in itself is unconditioned."[51] By faith, Buber means *emunah* and not *pistis*.

As we noticed in the previous chapter, Brunner rejects an intellectualistic understanding of *pistis* and sees it rather as "obedience-in-trust." In an excursus dealing with Buber's *Two Types of Faith*,[52] Brunner acknowledges his "tremendous service to theology" and expresses the conviction that the Christian can accept "with unmixed gratitude" all that Buber says about the Old Testament and the message of Jesus, even though Brunner adds a word of qualification at each point. But Brunner strongly objects to Buber's thesis that the Pauline and Johannine concepts of faith represent another type of faith from that which is found in the Old Testament and in the message of Jesus.

But criticism of Buber has not come solely from Christian sources. Buber's understanding of the Law (Torah) has evoked a negative reaction within Judaism.

[50] Buber, *Two Types of Faith*, p. 7.
[51] *Ibid.*, p. 9.
[52] Brunner, *The Christian Doctrine of the Church, Faith, and the Consummation*, pp. 159-62.

Buber refuses to admit any form of direct relationship between revelation and the Law (Torah) of Judaism and its traditions and regulations. The Jewish Law, according to Buber, is not essential to the Jewish tradition, and legalism may be a means of escape from personal responsibility under God.[53] The Torah is basically instruction, not laws. "It includes laws, and laws are indeed its vigorous objectivizations, but the Torah itself is essentially not law." [54] Our tendency to understand the term "law" in the objective sense, *nomos,* is a source of confusion because it tends to obscure the dynamic quality inhering in the Torah by virtue of its being the Word of God. Not objective commandment, not subjective volition, but personal relation with God is the source of obligation, and the Torah is not to be thought of as a body of laws.

Having pointed out that Buber insists that the Torah is basically not laws but instruction, we must add that he does not mean instruction in the sense of teaching general, timeless truths. For example, Buber insists that the Decalogue is erroneously construed as "the catechism of the Hebrews in the Mosaic period." [55] Revelation is not a source of timeless truths but concerns only the person himself "in his particular situation, and not in any general way." [56] The Decalogue is not really grasped by those who see it merely as enunciating moral truths, but only by those "who literally felt it as having been addressed to them themselves; only those, that is, who experienced that first one's state of being addressed as though they themselves were being addressed." [57] It was not God but Moses who hewed out

[53] Quoted in Friedman, *Martin Buber,* p. 262.
[54] Buber, *Two Types of Faith,* p. 57.
[55] Martin Buber, *Moses* (New York: East & West Library, 1946), p. 130.
[56] Buber, *Between Man and Man,* p. 80.
[57] Buber, *Moses,* p. 130.

the stone tablets of the Law in order that there might be a continuing testimony to what had been revealed to him. The function of the tables of the Law, according to Buber, "is to make present unto the generations of Israel forever what had once become word; that is, to set it before them as something spoken to them in this very hour." [58] It is not truth but the possibility of relation that is preserved by the Torah.

The most forceful critic of Buber's view is Franz Rosenzweig, "the rediscoverer of classical Judaism." [59] Like Buber he believes the Law is not a past event which "becomes increasingly past" but is held in memory in such a way as to be "eternally present." However, for Rosenzweig, the term "Torah" "designates both teaching and law as one." He insists that "only in the commandment can the voice of him who commands be heard." [60] It seemed inevitable that in spite of strong similarities with Buber he would clash with Buber's advocacy of freedom from the Law. For Buber resists the legalistic interpretation of the Torah as staunchly as he does the moralistic.

Although Rosenzweig initiated the controversy, he emphasized the wide area of agreement between Buber and himself. He highly commended Buber's formulation of the goals of Jewish learning for breaking down the rigid distinction between the essential and nonessential and thus opening up new vistas. He commends Buber's insight in developing a principle of selection for dealing with the new range of subject matter. The subject matter of teaching *(Lernstoff)* is subject to the test of whether or not it can become teaching

[58] *Ibid.*, p. 140.

[59] N. N. Glatzer, "Introduction," in Franz Rosenzweig's *On Jewish Learning,* ed. by N. N. Glatzer (New York: Schocken Books, 1955), p. 18.

[60] Franz Rosenzweig, *Franz Rosenzweig: His Life and Thought,* ed. by N. N. Glatzer (New York: Schocken Books, 1953), p. 300. See also p. 245.

(Lehre), i.e., whether or not the teaching can become an inner power for one who commits himself to it.[61]

However, Rosenzweig laments that Buber failed to make a similar contribution to Judaism in his treatment of the Law. Rosenzweig's concern has been described as being "to find the means of possessing the deed of Judaism in the same living fashion in which Buber has shown the thought of Judaism could be grasped." [62] He based his argument on an analogy to Buber's concept of teaching contending that content must become inner power.[63] He advocated the view that codified law *(Gesetz)* must be transformed into the immediacy of commandment *(Gebot)*, which must in turn be transformed into deed or living reality *(Heutigkeit)*.[64] Silberman gives this analysis: "The decision to act is the response not to an external demand that one act but to an internal recognition that one can act." [65] Rosenzweig is concerned to identify the old Jewish Law with the new living law.[66] Glatzer reminds us, in view of the "strictly undogmatic and apparently liberal approach" of Rosenzweig, that his actual purpose is to elevate the Law and to reestablish the connection between revelation and regulations, even those of minute importance.[67] Rosenzweig was raising a central issue in

---

[61] Franz Rosenzweig, *On Jewish Learning,* pp. 75-76.

[62] Silberman, *A People and its Faith,* p. 141.

[63] Buber rejects the analogy on the basis that there is a qualitative difference between deed and experience (we can atone for our deeds, but not for our experiences), and that our responsibility for what we have done or left undone is different from that for what we have learned or left unlearned (Martin Buber, "Revelation and Law," in Rosenzweig's *On Jewish Learning,* p. 115). Rosenzweig's rejoinder is that there is not an analogy between learning and doing but between thinking and doing, and that we can repent of our thoughts (Franz Rosenzweig, *Ibid.,* p. 116).

[64] *Ibid.,* p. 85.

[65] Silberman, *A People and its Faith,* p. 142.

[66] Rosenzweig, *On Jewish Learning,* p. 87.

[67] Glatzer, "Introduction," *On Jewish Learning,* p. 21. Cf. Silberman, *A People and its Faith,* p. 141.

Judaism and seemed to have a mixture of determination and confidence that Buber would assent to his views.

Rosenzweig did not ask much from Buber, but got less. Rosenzweig would have been satisfied with "a reverential nod towards the Law," in Silberman's terms.[68] Buber did not alter his position in the slightest and often showed a reluctance to discuss the issue, although considerable correspondence did ensue. Buber did express his agreement with that which follows from Rosenzweig's premises but refused to accept the premises themselves. He especially objected to the premise that revelation is a formulation of law, and insisted rather that it is "the unmediated word of God directed to a specific hour of life." He says that it is impossible for him to accept jointly both the Law and the Word of God.[69] Rosenzweig met this rebuff by urging that the difference between their views is minimal, chiefly by insisting that "even for him who observes the Law, revelation is not what you call law-giving." [70] Buber replied that Rosenzweig has not fully understood the difference between them and has failed to appreciate the fact that the transformation from revelation to commandment *(Gebot)* is an act of man.[71] In a later letter he remarked that "though man is a law-receiver, God is not a law giver," and therefore the Law has only personal, not universal, validity.[72] Rosenzweig disclaimed any notion of God as a law-giver, but insisted that God commands and that man is at fault when he legalizes and systematizes God's commandments instead of receiving them with "fear and trembling." [73] In spite of his persistent and determined efforts,

[68] Silberman, *A People and its Faith,* p. 141.
[69] Buber, "Revelation and Law," *On Jewish Learning,* pp. 111-12.
[70] Rosenzweig, *On Jewish Learning,* p. 113.
[71] Buber, *On Jewish Learning,* p. 114.
[72] *Ibid.,* p. 115.
[73] Rosenzweig, *On Jewish Learning,* p. 116.

Rosenzweig failed to induce Buber to make even the slightest concession.

Although he attempted to minimize the difference between his views and Buber's, Rosenzweig actually had the effect of highlighting and dramatizing them. Glatzer remarks that the letters between Rosenzweig and Buber show that beneath their friendship there lay "an abysmal difference of opinion." [74] Silberman remarks that the "magnitude" of the issue "overshadows the tension" between the two combatants.[75] Both men stress the importance of the personal relationship with God for vital religious life. Rosenzweig wants to buttress this with an external, objective Law; Buber, on the other hand, insists that any attempt to buttress it is to crush it. Revelation has no existence beyond the moment and finds no expression outside the relationship of a person with the eternal Thou—this is Buber's stand, and he cannot be lured, coaxed, or cajoled into the slightest equivocation of it. This radical repudiation of all impersonal elements in divine-human encounter is unnecessarily severe and limiting, and as we shall see Buber and Brunner cannot adhere strictly to it in practice.

Duration of Revelation

Buber attacked the notion that revelation, once given, endured, and replaced it with the concept of transitory revelation. If revelation comes through the transmission of propositions, then it consists in timeless truths. But if, as Buber contends, revelation comes through encounter, then, like the encounter itself, it can exist only as a thing of the moment. The true prophet is not the proclaimer of an immutable decree, but rather he "speaks into the power of decision lying in the

---

[74] Glatzer, "Introduction," *On Jewish Learning,* p. 21.
[75] Silberman, *A People and its Faith,* p. 142.

moment, and in such a way that his message of disaster just touches this power." [76] The future is not predetermined, for man is free and his personal decisions influence the future.

No one can decree once and for all the nature of our responsibility toward God, for "the one direction of the hour towards God" is continually changing. Neither without nor within can we find an immutable decree.

Certainly the relation of faith is no book of rules which can be looked up to discover what is to be done now, in this very hour. I experience what God desires of me for this hour—so far as I do experience it—not earlier than *in* the hour. But even then it is not given me to experience it except by answering before God for this hour as *my* hour, by carrying out the responsibility for it towards him as much as I can.[77]

The word from God cannot be looked up in a dictionary; indeed, it has just become word, yet it demands an answer. The answer, however inadequate, is a proper answer if it is the person's own answer for his hour. Parroting secondhand answers is not adequate. The person may, of course, get direction from the group, but the final decision must be his own, else he has surrendered the responsibility that is essential to the I-Thou relation.[78]

Buber changed the revelation from something static that can be taken out and looked at whenever we desire and made it vital and dynamic. And yet, by giving revelation life, Buber also exposed it to the threat of death.

Buber argues that man's desire for security is the cause of

[76] Buber, *The Prophetic Faith,* p. 103.
[77] Buber, *Between Man and Man,* p. 68. Similarly, Viktor Frankl argues that the meaning of life, like the "best move in chess," is relative to one's situation, which is constantly changing (*Man's Search for Meaning,* tr. by Ilse Lasch [Boston: Beacon, 1963], p. 110). Cf. Harold E. Hatt, "Existential Analysis and Logotherapy," *Encounter,* Summer, 1965, 330-39.
[78] Buber, *Between Man and Man,* pp. 68-69.

his attempt to make revelation enduring. He speaks of objectifying revelation as one of the arts of man's "craze for security." Man "desires a continuity in space and time of possession of God." He wants to see the confirmation of meaning "stretched out as something that can be continually taken up and handled, a continuum unbroken in space and time that insures his life at every point and moment." He describes the degeneration that occurs as a result of this unholy desire for an unreal security on the part of man. "At first faith, set in time, completes the acts of relation; but gradually it replaces them. Resting in belief in an *It* takes the place of the continually renewed movement of the being towards concentration and going out to the relation." He decries the fact that the "fighter" who knows what it is to be remote from God, as well as near to him, becomes transformed into the man who is unshaken in his assurance of the continual watch care of the deity on his behalf.[79] Buber is dismayed at this because he feels that such behavior is quite unbecoming to one who possesses the potentiality of entering into an I-Thou relation with God, which, though not permanent, is immeasurably richer and deeper.

Buber considers man's desire for community to be a further cause of his attempt to make revelation enduring. Man is not satisfied by "the 'solitude' of the *I* before the *Thou.*" In his desire for community man makes God the object of a cult, but in so doing, he makes degeneration of the cult inevitable.

The cult, too, completes at first the acts of relation, in adjusting in a spatial context of great formative power the living prayer, the immediate saying of the *Thou,* and in linking it with the life of the senses. It, too, gradually replaces the acts of relation, when the personal prayer is no longer supported, but displaced, by the

[79] Buber, *Between Man and Man,* p. 18; *I and Thou,* p. 113.

communal prayer, and when the act of the being, since it admits no rule, is replaced by ordered devotional exercises.[80]

By way of contrast, Buber insists that "the only authentic assurance of continuity" consists in the daily attempt of each person to realize God anew in the world. By surrounding God with cultic ritual and apparatus, we do not preserve, but smother, our relation with him. By freeing God (i.e., allowing him to remain free) from all such confinements, we perpetuate the possibility of vital contact with him.[81]

Many contemporary theologians have agreed with Buber that the desire for a permanent revelation is ignoble; yet they are also impressed by the strong historical note in Christianity and feel that this emphasis cannot be surrendered. As a result, considerable effort has been expended to introduce the personal element within a historical setting.

Assurance of Revelation

Buber attacked the notion that revelation, once given, may be known with objective certainty, and replaced this with the notion of personal assurance. Since revelation comes through encounter and is a thing of the present moment only, our assurance concerning it must be subjective and transitory. To give up the hope for certainty and to take the risk of faith "does not insure the truth for us; but it, and it alone, leads us to where the breath of truth is to be felt." [82]

Buber claims that with regard to Luther's refusal of fellowship with Zwingli and Calvin's part in the death of Servetus, he is unable to form a judgment (though one would have to be dull-witted indeed not to notice the implicit

[80] Buber, *I and Thou*, p. 114.
[81] *Ibid.*
[82] Buber, *Between Man and Man*, p. 71. Cf. *Ibid.*: "There is no certainty. There is only a chance."

strain of criticism), because, unlike them, he does not subscribe to the belief that the Word of God can be clearly known and hence ought to be exclusively advocated. Buber insists that the difference in point of view is not merely subjective, nor does it result from the fact that men today are weak in faith. Rather, it grows out of the changed understanding of the relation between man and God and between man and fellowmen.[83]

As for his position, Buber claims that "the Word of God crosses my vision like a falling star to whose fire the meteorite will bear witness without making it light up for me, and I myself can only bear witness to the light but not produce the stone and say 'This is it.' " Buber also uses a physiological analogy to express his view. "Religion as risk, which is ready to give itself up, is the nourishing stream of the arteries; as system, possessing, assured, and assuring, religion which believes in religion is the veins' blood, which ceases to circulate." Just as we may use morality to hide from us the face of our fellowman, in like manner we may use dogma to hide from us the face of God.[84]

Buber removed revelation from the cold world of objects and established it within the warmth of personal relationship. But by bringing revelation into contact with the warmth of personality he dissolved the possibility of cold, objective certainty concerning it.

Buber feels that we can expect no stronger confidence than that of personal assurance. He says that theology which pretends to be demonstrable assertion is, rather, "a questionable type of philosophy." God will not corroborate the true prophet's pronouncement, and in this sense God's revelation "is nothing but a different form of hiding his face." [85]

[83] *Ibid.*, p. 7.
[84] *Ibid.*, pp. 7, 18.
[85] Buber, *Eclipse of God,* p. 59; *The Prophetic Faith,* p. 177.

We are not completely without guidance, but we cannot substitute the guidance offered by others for personal decision, and we have no right to expect the finger that points the way should be that of God. The result is that "there is not the slightest assurance that our decision is right in any but a personal way." Although God gives the situation to which I have to answer, I cannot expect that he should grant me the answer or any part of it. Whose, then, is the finger that points the way? It is the finger of "conscience," but not in the usual sense of the term, i.e., not "the routine conscience, which is to be used, is being used and worn out, the play-on-the-surface conscience." Rather it is "the unknown conscience in the ground of being." Such a conscience operates in the I-Thou relation and shares in its transitory character, and thus "needs to be discovered ever anew." The assurance that this conscience gives is spoken of as "personal certainty" and "uncertain certainty." Buber would rather be uncertainly certain than certainly certain, for the former means being in relation, and for Buber relation is the pearl of great price.[86]

Having for the most part given up for some time objective proofs (such as the arguments from miracles and prophecy), Christian theologians have striven to formulate some means of inner certainty which is consistent with the strains of strong faith and hope in the Scripture. The contemporary Christian may not enjoy as much of a "sure hope" as did his predecessors in the faith, but his loss in this area is more than compensated for in the fact that he exercises a more "lively hope" than did his forbears in the faith.

Buber's concept of revelation has confronted every contemporary Christian thinker. Wolf does not pay him too high a compliment when he says: "Whether or not the Buber terminology is used, his analysis accurately describes the

[86] Buber, *Between Man and Man*, p. 69.

element without which revelation is not revelation but simply talk about revelation." [87] Baillie exclaims: "How far we have travelled from the New Testament when we think of God's revelation as being of such a kind as to put a strain on the memory!" [88] But, due largely to the influence of Martin Buber, we have begun to travel back after having strayed so far. Despite the unquestioned value of the emphasis upon encounter, it will still be our duty to consider whether it yields an adequate understanding of how revelation yields doctrine.

[87] Wolf, *Man's Knowledge of God*, p. 83.
[88] Baillie, *The Idea of Revelation in Recent Thought*, p. 30—said in reference to a line in the preface to the catechism prepared by the Council of Trent, Quaestio, xii.

4. Brunner's Concept of Revelation

The consequence of Brunner's insistence (examined in Chapter 2) that the truth of revelation is personal encounter is his denial that it is propositional. In this chapter we will deal with some of the implications of Brunner's concept of nonpropositional theology, and the explanation offered by Buber and Brunner to describe how revelation yields doctrine.

The Status of the Bible

From Brunner's point of view the Bible is not revelation, but it does reveal.[1] Brunner states quite firmly that the inspiration of the Bible "is not *the* revelation but one of the forms

---

[1] It is true that Brunner has said that the Bible "does not only speak of the revelation; it is itself the revelation" (*Revelation and Reason,* p. 21). But in this context he is thinking of the Bible as a written form of the church's proclamation or witness. Hence, he is thinking of the Bible as revelation in the sense of activity rather than in the substantive sense. So it is still true that for Brunner the Bible is not revelation (substantive), but it does reveal (verb).

of revelation"—i.e., the written form. The revelation, in written form, is found only in the Bible and not in any other religious book. As the written form of revelation, the Bible, when it speaks of revelation, "points beyond itself to an event, to which indeed it bears witness, but which is not the Bible itself." [2]

The fault of orthodoxy is to put the Bible itself, *qua* book, in the place of revelation, confusing "the fact of revelation with the witness to the fact." A connection between the two is necessary, but it is erronous to make them identical. The tragedy of this error is that the Bible absorbs the "passionate interest" of men instead of directing it toward Christ.[3]

In spite of the danger of equating the two, the church must continue to speak of the Bible as "Word of God." In so doing she testifies to "the fundamental truth of the Christian faith, namely, that in these books the historical self-manifestation of God is offered to faith in an incomparable, decisive, and unique manner." [4] The Bible may be spoken of as "the Word of God" because God has chosen to use it to reveal himself to man.[5] Brunner uses the analogy of a gramaphone record. Incidental noises are unavoidable, but this medium makes "the master's voice" audible.[6] Indeed, so important is the role of the Bible that "no Christian faith can either arise or be preserved" which ignores it.[7] By denying the Bible the status of revelation, Brunner is by no means denying its revelatory function as a witness to revelation.

Testifying to the witness of the Bible is the witness of the church, and the witness of the Spirit confirms the

---

[2] Brunner, *Revelation and Reason,* p. 12.
[3] Brunner, *The Mediator,* p. 34.
[4] Brunner, *Revelation and Reason,* p. 118.
[5] *Ibid.,* p. 135.
[6] Emil Brunner, *Our Faith,* tr. by John W. Rilling (London: SCM Press, 1949), pp. 19-20.
[7] Brunner, *Revelation and Reason,* p. 118.

witness of the Bible and the church. Unlike the prophets and apostles, we are not given revelation directly but receive it indirectly through the instrumentality of witness to the revelation. The witness of the Scripture is basic. However, very few come to a living faith directly through reading the Bible, but rather through the witness of the church. The vast majority are won through "the witness of living persons, through the *viva vox ecclesiae.*" The church is both the community of believers and the body which produces faith. The church is "not only *communio* but also *mater fidelium.* . . . Christians are not only called to *be* disciples but to *make* disciples." The church proclaims its message not solely through the spoken word but also through the visible word of the Sacrament, which is a highly significant action of the church because it shows that Christ is more than can be expressed in words. Confirming the witness given through the Bible and the church is the witness of the Spirit. The authority of the Bible, or our assurance of its truth, rests on the inner speaking of Christ through the Holy Spirit so that the person is convinced that this is God's Word to him. Although we must receive the Word of God indirectly, we can be assured that God has spoken to us.[8]

The doctrine of verbal inspiration is firmly and vigorously rejected by Brunner. He is convinced that the Logos theologians, who equated the Bible with the Word of God, "infected Christian thought with their sterile intellectualism." [9] Although such a transformation of the Gospel is seriously damaging, it is nonetheless difficult to discern since it affects not merely articles of doctrine but the entire doctrinal system. Transformations of this nature are likened to "the sign before an algebraic paranthesis or the constant factors in a physics formula."

[8] Brunner, *Revelation and Reason,* pp. 118 ff, 136 ff, 161 ff.
[9] Brunner, *The Christian Doctrine of God,* p. 28.

To track down such a presupposition—foreign, even contrary, to the Bible itself—is therefore as difficult as it is necessary: difficult because it cannot be discovered in a single article of doctrine but extends through the whole of it; necessary because it has alienated from its peculiar meaning the entirety of Christian doctrine. The "sickness," figuratively speaking, lies not in a localized abscess or in a deformed organ but, rather, in the corruption of the blood, which thus secretly spreads the corruption into all organs.[10]

Brunner is not daunted by the difficulty but presses forward to confirm the validity of his diagnosis.

To establish his point Brunner seeks to demonstrate that the source of the doctrine of verbal inspiration is extra-biblical, and that its effect is detrimental. He contends that the doctrine of verbal inspiration arose from a twofold misunderstanding, viz. "from an academic view of the nature of revelation," and "from a Judaistic understanding of the Bible." He insists that the Bible itself "does not give any occasion for this misunderstanding." [11]

However, once the Bible came to be regarded as the locus of divinely revealed propositions, then "everything depends upon the process of revelation as the transference of the infallible divine truth to the human system of doctrine," and it followed necessarily that the Bible must be considered infallible if it is to serve as the link between God and doctrine.[12] Brunner finds it "impossible to take this enviable shortcut"; but being aware of the "terrible consequences" to which it leads he does not really regret having to choose "the longer way." [13] The doctrine of verbal inspiration is not only "entirely inadequate as a definition of the New Testa-

---

[10] Brunner, *Truth as Encounter*, p. 68.
[11] Brunner, *Revelation and Reason*, p. 118.
[12] *Ibid.,* p. 9.
[13] Brunner, *The Christian Doctrine of God,* p. 28.

ment revelation," [14] but it is also "actually a breach of the Second Commandment: it is the deification of a creature, bibliolatry." [15] For Brunner verbal inspiration is thought of as sacrilegious, quite in contrast with those who consider it an essential doctrine.

The relation between the Bible and doctrine is much more tenuous for Brunner than for those who hold the orthodox view, but it is not severed. The New Testament is not itself "a book of doctrine, but it is a collection of apostolic confessions of faith and historical records which have been written down in order to awaken and strengthen faith." [16] Indeed, the apostolic witness is essential to our knowledge of Jesus as the Christ. Brunner considers it "a fact of the highest significance that the Bible contains nothing which, even in the most remote way, resembles either a 'catechism of Christian doctrine' or a textbook of dogmatics." Even the book of Romans, "which comes closest to a connected account of doctrine," does not bear such a resemblance.[17] And so, for Brunner, the Bible is primarily a book of human, and therefore fallible, testimonies.

Yet Brunner does not wish to express the view that the Bible is completely void of doctrine. He does insist, however, that such doctrine as is found in the Bible "contains a minimum of doctrinal reflection" as "an essential characteristic." [18] Doctrine is definitely not primary in Scripture, but it is involved nonetheless.

For even if God does not deliver a course of lectures in dogmatic theology or submit a creed to us, but addresses us, so on the other hand it is not to be denied that in his Word God gives us himself in no other way than that he says "something" to us. In other

[14] *Ibid.,* p. 32.
[15] Brunner, *Revelation and Reason,* p. 120.
[16] Brunner, *The Christian Doctrine of God,* p. 12.
[17] Brunner, *Revelation and Reason,* pp. 135, 149.
[18] Brunner, *The Christian Doctrine of God,* p. 39.

words, the Word of God contains doctrine in some way, and the faith which is the answer to prayer entails knowledge.[19]

And so, while the Bible does not teach theology, the testimonies of the Bible do contain varying degrees of intellectual and theological reflection.[20] Indeed, even the simplest prayer offered by a mother at her child's bedside "contains definite theological ideas." Such doctrinal elements within the Bible are a "form" of God's revelation, even though this form, like the man Jesus, "both reveals and conceals the eternal Son of God." [21] Moreover, the Bible, along with faith, is the source from which true doctrine "springs." [22] Consequently, the subject of theology consists of "the content of the biblical message and of faith." [23] The Bible is not, however, "the final court of appeal," for Jesus Christ alone is the ultimate authority; but while the Bible is not an *authority,* it is "the *source* of all that truth which possesses absolute authority." [24] Brunner feels that his deposition of the Bible from the status of authority to that of witness is not a demotion but the surrender of a vain and false claim. As authority the Bible is only a pretender, but as witness it is performing its true function in accordance with its nature and rank.

The Nature of Theology

Theology, as seen from Brunner's perspective, may be characterized as inadequate, but necessary, for faith, although subordinate to it. Theology is inadequate for the very simple reason that its tools are inadequate for the task that is set for

---

[19] Brunner, *Truth as Encounter,* p. 119. Cf. pp. 132-33.
[20] Brunner, *The Christian Doctrine of God,* p. 12.
[21] Brunner, *Revelation and Reason,* pp. 151-52.
[22] *Ibid.,* p. 420.
[23] *Ibid.,* p. 385.
[24] Brunner, *The Christian Doctrine of God,* p. 47.

it. Theology is an attempt to express by means of words that which cannot be expressed adequately by such means. God's Word is not a "static theory"; nor is it a Word "which man can manipulate as he chooses." [25] "Anyone whose faith is identical with 'belief in a creed' would be in a bad way! He would simply be holding a dead form without power or life." [26] The proclamation and teaching of the church is a human attempt to express divine truth.[27] It is always less than the message, since it is but the intellectual element separated from the existential whole of the divine address.[28] Even the apostles were aware that all their teaching can never "exhaust" the revelation, and that their words "are only continually renewed attempts to say 'it.' " This awareness accounts for the fact that they did not try "to construct a doctrinal 'standard,' " but rather set forth many formulations in an unceasing struggle to find a better form of expression.[29]

Although we must "take pains" in the effort to attain clarity of theological expression, "yet we must not imagine that we have really said 'it' when we have dissected and redefined our definitions a hundred times over." The church's expression of her faith is a "venture, and can never be more than provisional." The theologian's reach must always exceed his grasp.[30]

In spite of the fact that the theologian can never accomplish his task, it is necessary that he continue to exert effort to reach his unattainable goal. Theology protects the message of the church by defending the faith "from destructive mis-

---

[25] Brunner, *The Mediator,* p. 595.

[26] Brunner, *Revelation and Reason,* p. 159. In this discussion Brunner equates creedal confession with the formulation of the doctrinal (intellectual) aspect of the faith, and describes this as "a meager abstraction compared with the proclamation of the Gospel" *(Ibid).*

[27] *Ibid.,* p. 3.

[28] Brunner, *The Mediator,* p. 597.

[29] Brunner, *The Christian Doctrine of God,* p. 32.

[30] Brunner, *Revelation and Reason,* pp. 153, 158.

understanding." [31] Without theology the church would become merged with the world. Indeed, in one place Brunner
speaks of reflection upon revelation as the "first and most
urgent task" of the church.[32] In another, he speaks of teaching theology as a "holy vocation" of the church.[33] Even though
God's Word cannot be confined within human language, still
it does not come to us apart from this vehicle. Brunner is
quite emphatic that "we only come to the knowledge of Him
where definite words and statements about Him are made,
and expressed, and understood." [34] Of course, the doctrine
necessary for faith may be "an extraordinarily small
amount." [35] However, doctrine can never be completely
obviated.

Brunner speaks of doctrine as token (the means of convey-
ing the Reality) and framework (the abstract bearer of the
Reality), and says that these have a necessary, not an accidental, connection with the reality of the personal Presence.
As a consequence, "we can never separate the abstract framework from the personal Presence contained in it, although
certainly we must differentiate them." Since the relation between doctrine and the Word of God "is in the last analysis
incommensurable," it must suffice for us "to recognize that
an abysmal difference, and yet at the same time a necessary
connection, lies between the two." Brunner also speaks of
"the indissoluble sacramental connection between doctrine and
Word of God." Although the goal of theology is unattainable,
its pursuit is unavoidable.[36]

Actually Brunner goes a step further and says that not
only theology but also correct doctrine is necessary. He says

[31] Brunner, *The Mediator*, p. 594.
[32] Brunner, *Revelation and Reason*, p. 3.
[33] Brunner, *Truth as Encounter*, p. 178.
[34] Brunner, *Revelation and Reason*, p. 151.
[35] Brunner, *Truth as Encounter*, p. 140.
[36] *Ibid.*, pp. 132-34, 140, 178.

quite plainly: "Faith cannot exist apart from sound doctrine." No, not even the Word of God can create faith "apart from correct doctrine." Incorrect doctrine "points man in the wrong direction," with the result that neither can we find God nor he us. However, even though "the power" of the witness "depends precisely" upon doctrinal correctness, yet "it does not depend exclusively upon it." Correct doctrine is necessary but not sufficient. The church has thus been right in exercising great care about the purity of its doctrine but has not been right in having done so in a "one-sided, rigid way." Moreover, hazy doctrine, even though correct, is inadequate to perform the task of pointing to Christ. There is "nothing indefinite" about the faith of the church. Clarity and precision are necessary. "We must say quite *clearly:* Christ is the Truth. *he* is the content; he is the 'point' of all the preaching of the Church; but he is also really its *content.* The human word must point definitely to him and to him alone." Although theology is not "the basis or the root of the church," it is nevertheless "an organ of examination and clarification." [37]

Because the enemies and the attacks vary from time to time, it is necessary that the work of theology be carried on, even though the message which it seeks to defend remains the same.[38] The fact that the final goal of theology is unattainable should not deter its efforts to attain proximate goals.

Theologians must remember, however, that their work is subordinate. Theology is of instrumental, not intrinsic, value. Brunner describes dogma as a banner behind which the followers of Christ may rally; a password by which they may recognize one another; and a signpost indicating the path they are to pursue.[39] Each of these pictures suggests a subordinate or auxiliary role for theology.

[37] Brunner, *Revelation and Reason,* pp. 420, 151-53, 159, 155.
[38] Brunner, *The Mediator,* pp. 594-95.
[39] Brunner, *Revelation and Reason,* pp. 158-59.

The subordination of theology is clearly necessitated by the fact that ultimately theology depends on faith, not faith on theology. Theology serves faith as a wall of defense, a pointer, and a framework. Brunner warns that if this relationship is reversed, the wall of defense will kill, or at least almost stifle, that which it was supposed to protect. "The wood which was intended to support the tree has used up all the vital sap" when orthodoxy corrupts faith with its intellectualism.[40] Theology is not the object of faith but a pointer to the object of faith, which is Jesus Christ himself. So, faith is not directed toward doctrine but "skims past it, as it were, like a ball from the barrel of a gun, toward the goal. Or again, to use another metaphor, doctrine is the telescope through which we are to see him." Consequently, dogma is not "*credendum*" but "*creditum*," i.e., it is not an *edict* of what *must* be believed, but a confession of what *is* believed.[41] Theology, then, is a servant and must not seek to go beyond its subordinate role; for if it should do so, it would, in that very act, destroy its *raison d'être*. But if this is so, then theological activity does not create its truth through reflection on encounter but discovers propositional truth which is prior to or coincident with encounter. It is such a position that will be defended in the final chapter.

A further indication of the subordinate role of theology is that it is intelligible only to those who already believe. In speaking of dogma as a banner behind which the church may rally, Brunner declares that only those who are already followers can understand this banner, and that it is not a sign for the world but for the church. The church has a confession "*because* she believes, not *in order* to believe."[42]

[40] Brunner, *The Mediator,* p. 595.
[41] Brunner, *Revelation and Reason,* p. 156.
[42] *Ibid.,* p. 158.

The confession of faith is not the path that the Christian follows but the fence that marks off the right and left boundaries. As such, it is "like a good map; it is only 'legible' to one who knows the real Word." And so Brunner concludes that "only the believer can be taught by dogma." The reason for this is that the believer understands the statements of dogma to have been erected by believers who have preceded him on the path and have set up signals to halt at places where there is a danger of going astray. What they say to him is: " 'Do not pass beyond this sign!' But it is not the dogma which binds him, but the truth to which the dogma points." [43]

Dogma plays an important role, but only because faith has created a situation in which it may serve. "Not enough stress can be placed in the congregation upon doctrine and knowledge of doctrine; but the measure of doctrinal development that the individual and congregation can endure without suffering injury to their faith is always proportionate to the measure of practical realization of that faith." [44]

In his discussion of the subordinate role of theology, Brunner conceives of it as stating that which faith "knows." He implies a knowledge prior to, and independent of, theology, which theology in turn expresses, both clarifying and elaborating it. To me the most plausible explanation of the source of this knowledge, which is the material of theology, is that it is given in encounter.

Brunner is convinced that once the relation between the Word of God and doctrine is rightly understood, "there will hardly be room any longer for the view that the single thing which the church could do for the awakening of faith is the conceptual clarification of the Holy Scriptures." Hence Brunner rejects the view that catechetical instruction "is the best *way* to faith." The teaching of doctrine and the preaching of

[43] Brunner, *The Mediator*, pp. 597-98.
[44] Brunner, *Truth as Encounter*, pp. 178-79.

doctrinal sermons "normally belongs where there is already a confessional congregation, where the concern is no longer with establishing a believing congregation, but rather with strengthening faith and deepening knowledge of faith." [45] Doctrine is not only subordinate to faith; it may be quite unintelligible to those who are outside faith.

Moreover, contrary to popular notion, theology is subordinate to preaching, except, of course, doctrinal preaching, which does not differ essentially from the teaching of doctrine. Under the influence of Greek intellectualism this truth was obscured "almost from the very outset." Because Christ is the truth, witness to him (preaching) is primary and talking about him (doctrine) is secondary. The preaching of the church, along with "every personal, challenging proclamation of the Christian message," is central, standing "between the witness of the Apostles to Christ and the doctrine of the church, its dogma, catechism, and theology." [46] Compared with the proclamation of the Gospel, the confession is "always a meager abstraction." [47] Hence, Brunner has no hesitation in naming proclamation, rather than doctrine, as the "primary commission of the church." Even though preaching "must always have a doctrinal content," it is definitely "something other than doctrine." Preaching is "faith-awakening, faith-furthering, faith-wooing address." It may be distinguished from doctrine as having a "prophetic" rather than a "didactic" character.[48] "The revelation of God must be *told,* not taught." Doctrine is valid only as it serves the proclamation of the Gospel, but when it replaces proclamation, "Greek thought triumphs over the thought of the Bible." [49] Theology is explication of the great words of

[45] *Ibid.,* pp. 179-81.
[46] Brunner, *Revelation and Reason,* pp. 149-50.
[47] *Ibid.,* p. 159.
[48] Brunner, *Truth as Encounter,* pp. 178-79.
[49] Brunner, *Revelation and Reason,* p. 201.

the Bible and reflection upon that which has been revealed through and about Jesus Christ, which is carried on "in such a way that both the preaching of the church and the deepening and clarification of faith itself will be served by it." [50] A doctrinal cónfession may be considered a "norm of preaching" in the sense that "to preach something different will not create the faith which the church possesses." [51] Theology is subservient to and an instrument of preaching.

Brunner further claims that when doctrine is isolated from the Word of God the consequence is legalism. When doctrine is so isolated, man is not in relation with God himself but with truths about God. Such a faith is "a deception, a facsimile of the true faith, a counterfeit bill which has exactly the same markings as a good one, but the signature, the certification, is lacking." Such " 'credo-credo faith,' " as Brunner terms it, "is a tragic blight that lies over the whole history of the church." [52] The church has so often believed that "it need only pile doctrine upon doctrine, without troubling about practical results and without noticing that in this way it kills souls instead of awakening them to a true life." [53] Brunner insists that any demand of God, other than the demand "that I should let him give me life, is moralistic legalism." [54] Overemphasis on doctrine has been achieved at the expense of ethics, and the church has shown greater concern for orthodoxy than for a genuine sense of discipleship on the part of its members. As a consequence of the overemphasis on the intellectual aspects, the ethical aspects were either ignored, or legalized, which to Brunner "is just as bad." [55] Dogmatic orthodoxy is labeled as the worst foe

[50] *Ibid.*, p. 385.
[51] *Ibid.*, p. 159.
[52] Brunner, *Truth as Encounter,* pp. 138-39.
[53] *Ibid.*, p. 179. Cf. p. 164.
[54] Brunner, *God and Man,* p. 66. Cf. p. 88.
[55] Brunner, *Revelation and Reason,* p. 154.

of morality.[56] In such an atmosphere the activities of the Holy Spirit are known because the scripture teaches them, rather than because they are actually experienced.[57] In orthodoxy, faith, rather than love, is primary. "If only your support of doctrine is clear and unequivocal, you are a Christian—however you may have disposed of the matter of love." [58] Failure to see doctrine in its proper perspective is not only latent with theoretical errors but also with practical disasters.

The Unity of Revelation

Brunner feels that behind the varying Christian doctrines that have been formulated there is a unity of revelation at its source. Although there are "manifold doctrines," there is but "one truth of Christ." Brunner believes in the unity of revelation in the sense that its source is single and its truth is one. However, "the divine Truth is a light which cannot be received by the human mind without being refracted." Since the church's task is to proclaim the truth of Christ, it must carry on a continual search "for the one Light of Truth within these refractions," and dogmatics is the science which it employs in this endeavor.[59] And Brunner adheres to a unity of revelation received through a diversity of forms and considers it the role of theology to make continually the vain, but necessary, attempt to go from the latter to the former.

Brunner, however, considers doctrinal variety a *necessitatum* rather than a *desideratum*. Brunner has no hesitation that if Christian doctrine were forced to choose between the attitude of "tolerance" and "relativism" on one hand, and "dogmatic

---

[56] Brunner, *The Mediator*, p. 598.
[57] Brunner, *Truth as Encounter*, p. 139.
[58] *Ibid.*, p. 167.
[59] Brunner, *The Christian Doctrine of God*, p. 13.

intolerance" on the other, it would have to choose the latter; but he is quick to brand this a false alternative.[60] Brunner might not put it quite this strongly, but the suggestion seems to be that he would like to choose the latter but simply cannot. The evidence which thwarts his desire is too strong to be ignored.

Even within the Bible itself, there is not a unity of doctrine but rather a "unity of the divine purpose in saving history." [61] Such a unity not only allows for but necessitates differences in other respects. When we turn to the larger sphere of church history, we are again forcibly struck by the fact that "various forms of widely divergent 'Christian doctrine' have always existed within the Christian Church." [62] Although the church has often had the confidence that a unity of doctrine could be attained, it has never been able to realize this hope.

Some continue to hope that we may yet attain a unity of doctrine, but Brunner considers this dream of orthodoxy vain. The notion of revelation as encounter does not permit the step from unity of revelation to unity of doctrine. "Where the effort is made to conceive the unity of revelation as a unity of doctrine—as all orthodoxy tries to do—there, without noticing it, history is changed into idea, and the Living God of the Bible becomes the absolute Being of speculative philosophy." [63] The unity of revelation does not imply a unity of doctrine, but only a unity of source which unites varying ways of thought on the basis that they converge in a common center. As a matter of fact, Brunner suggests that so-called "Orthodoxy" is really a misnomer, for "orthodox" merely means teaching which points in the right direction.

[60] *Ibid.*, p. 50.
[61] Brunner, *Revelation and Reason,* p. 197. Cf. p. 195: "a unity of divine revealing action."
[62] Brunner, *The Christian Doctrine of God,* p. 50.
[63] Brunner, *Revelation and Reason,* p. 201.

"Right," or sound, doctrine will thus be understood literally as "rightly directed," rightly orientated doctrine; this will never mean that the actual truth under discussion will be equated with its doctrinal expression; it only means that "right" doctrine points, definitely and clearly, in the *right* direction. "Right," or sound, doctrine is not a system of fixed doctrines, standing in a row, side by side; but it is doctrine in a "radial" sense, pointing towards a Center. . . . The soundness of theological doctrine and ideas depends upon their direction, upon the single-mindedness with which they point to Him.[64]

The cherished ideal of a "closed theological system" is abandoned by Brunner as an "illusion." [65] But although doctrines vary, the source from which they spring and the truth which they attest is one.

The Role of Reason

It is difficult to choose a word to describe the relation between revelation and reason in Brunner's thought, both because of the complexity of the relation and also because Brunner's position has been shifting. As a general rule, but subject to much exception, Brunner's later works make a greater concession to the role of reason in theology. However, the difference is one of degree not of kind. DeWolf remarks that Brunner's "concessions to the rationalists are especially noteworthy in *Revelation and Reason.* But they have not erased the influences of his earlier, more extreme utterances." [66] Whatever term we employ to describe this

[64] *Ibid.,* p. 157.
[65] *Ibid.*
[66] L. Harold DeWolf, *The Religious Revolt Against Reason* (New York: Harper & Brothers, 1949), p. 27. DeWolf feels that there is a tendency in recent theology toward a higher evaluation of reason ("Changing Emphases in Recent Theology," *The Journal of Bible and Religion,* April, 1955, pp. 105-6.

aspect of Brunner's thought, it will be necessary to exercise care in understanding it.

The term "dialectical" is used here and is to be understood largely in the Hegelian sense of merging thesis and antithesis into a synthesis. Brunner's thought is far from having a Hegelian orientation, but in at least this area we may detect a faint Hegelian echo. Objectivism-subjectivism is a "fatal antithesis" for the church, and the "God-given power of the Reformation" consisted in the fact that the church was enabled "to find the secret of moving both between and beyond these extremes." [67] Orthodoxy gets off on the wrong foot by applying the general concept of truth to revelation "instead of surmounting this understanding of truth by means of revelation." [68] Every theoretical understanding of revelation "is in its very inception a misunderstanding," for the Word which comes as a challenge cannot be appreciated from the spectator's standpoint.[69] Something can be said on both the credit and debit side for objectivism and subjectivism,[70] but the church dare not choose one or the other, nor a combination of both. Rather she must take account of both and then forge ahead of them, uniting a duality of logically contradictory elements in a paradoxical unity. The truth which the church is concerned is not basically rational but basically personal.

Before considering further the concept of paradox, we

[67] Brunner, *Truth as Encounter*, p. 75.

[68] *Ibid.*, p. 164.

[69] Emil Brunner, *The Theology of Crisis* (New York: Scribner's, 1935), pp. 37-38.

[70] Objectivism insists that God's act is prior to and independent of any human act, with the result that it preserves to some extent "what may be called the substance of the church." Subjectivism insists that "God's free rule of the Spirit can be received by man only in an equally free spiritual act," with the result that its protest against objectivism is often the cause of the blossoming of biblical truth. On the other hand, objectivism leads to torpidity and subjectivism to dissolution (Brunner, *Truth as Encounter*, pp. 174-75).

must call attention to Brunner's insistence that he does not mean to do away entirely with the object-subject antithesis, for rational thought must be carried on in terms of this correlation. In *Truth as Encounter* Brunner's thesis is that the object-subject antithesis leads to falsification when applied to revelation.[71] He is careful to add that the object-subject antithesis is nonetheless "indispensable for natural-rational knowing," and that to give it up would necessitate a cessation of thinking. Brunner then proceeds in detail to reject both objectivism and subjectivism for the understanding of revelation, and to insist, rather, on the dialectical principle.[72] He expresses his concern to avoid "the Scylla of an already existing Orthodoxy," but also to exercise care lest he "give way to the Charybdis of a new Pietism." [73] God reveals himself as a Thou, in radical contrast to anything objective; and the human response of trust is "something quite other than subjectivity." [74] Brunner will not joust with the "Object-Subject horseman" elsewhere, but whenever he enters the field of faith Brunner tilts his lance against him.

When the church does forge ahead and take possession of her "Promised Land," she will find herself living in a land flowing not only with milk and honey but also with paradox. There are some who feel that paradox should be likened to milk because of the nourishment it provides for the life of faith, and with honey because of the sweetness it contributes.

---

[71] His statement is: "*that the use of the objective-subject antithesis in understanding the truth of faith* and furthermore in the church generally is by no means self-evident; on the contrary, it *is a disastrous misunderstanding* which affects the entire content of Christian doctrine and also operates fatally in the practice of the church, most severely impairing the proclamation of the Word and faith among the fellowship. *The Biblical understanding of truth cannot be grasped through the object-subject antithesis: on the contrary, it is falsified through it*" (*Ibid.*, p. 69. Cf. p. 85 for a shorter statement of the same thesis).

[72] *Ibid.*, pp. 70-76.

[73] *Ibid.*, p. 83.

[74] *Ibid.*, p. 109.

Others, however feel that the analogy is more aptly based on the liquidity of the former and the stickiness of the latter.

For his part, Brunner insists that throughout her history the church has been aware of the fact that her beliefs are paradoxical and absurd from the rational point of view. "The hallmark of logical inconsistency clings to all genuine pronouncements of faith." Brunner remarks that in times of strength, the church has emphasized the opposition between reason and revelation; in times of weakness, she has stressed apology; but he insists that in explaining continuity and discontinuity the church has always included reason within the bounds of revelation, and never revelation within the bounds of reason.[75] And yet, Brunner remarks that although "there are plenty of books with the title *Reason and Revelation*," his is the first to indicate a reversal of this order of inquiry in its title.[76] Brunner finds "dialectically oscillating" principles in the Bible.[77] He describes the epistemological principles of the Reformation as dialectical and explains: "That is, its form of expression was never the use of one concept, but always two logically contradictory ones." It is important to note that these contradictory concepts are "understood and experienced" as a unity and not as a duality.[78] The inebriate often receives a dual image of one physical object, but Brunner's version of the "God intoxicated" man is able to understand and experience two logically contradictory concepts as one.

The concept of two kinds of knowledge and two kinds of truth is fundamental in Brunner's thought. The importance

[75] Emil Brunner, *The Philosophy of Religion*, tr. by A. J. D. Farrer and Bertram Lee Woolf (New York: Scribner's, 1937), pp. 55-56.

[76] *Revelation and Reason*, p. ix.

[77] Brunner, *Truth as Encounter*, p. 82.

[78] *Ibid.*, pp. 75-76. He cites as examples the "paradoxical unity of Word and Spirit, of historical revelation and God's contemporary presence, of 'Christ for us' and 'Christ in us.'"

of this concept to Brunner's system is indicated by the number of phrases he employs to express it.

Such distinctions as the knowledge of address and the knowledge of reflection *(Anruf und Reflexions-Erkenntnis)*, theoretical knowledge and the knowledge of faith *(Theoretischeerkenntnis und Glaubenserkenntnis)*, God and world truth *(Gott-und-Weltwahrheit)*, personal and abstract truth *(personhafte und sachlische Wahrheit)*, rational truth and truth which is communicated *(Vernunft-und-Mitteilungswahrheit)*, objective and subjective truth *(objecktive und subjektive Wahrheit)*, are scattered *passim* through Brunner's writings, all having the same fundamental connotation.[79]

But Brunner is not resurrecting the medieval notion of double truth. He says quite unequivocally: "From the outset and most decidedly, we would reject the very notion of a double truth as dishonest. What is recognized as valid in science cannot be untrue for faith." [80] It is not only dishonest but disastrous, for "dual truth amounts to no truth at all." [81] Revelation and reason are quite different approaches for Brunner, but they "possess one common element: They both claim truth." [82] The difference is a matter of "proportion," i.e., there is a continuum.[83] However, the method by which the truth is gained affects the very nature of the truth itself, and it is on this fact that Brunner bases his disjunction.

Knowledge and truth may be sought through the exercise of reason following either of the alternate routes of science and philosophy, or through personal encounter. Let us briefly examine each of these methods of seeking truth and knowledge.

The truth of science grows out of immediate experience.

---

[79] Jewett, *Emil Brunner's Concept of Revelation*, p. 88 n.
[80] Brunner, *Revelation and Reason*, pp. 204-5.
[81] Brunner, *The Philosophy of Religion*, p. 55.
[82] Brunner, *Revelation and Reason*, p. 362.
[83] *Ibid.*, p. 383.

The man of average education usually thinks of truth in these terms. For the scientist truth is basically something to be found largely by observation and measurement, and the main value of scientific method is that it allows man to control things according to his purposes.[84] Brunner respects the findings of science and is quite censorious toward Orthodoxy for its obstinate rejection of scientific findings.[85] However, he considers science "superficial" in the sense of dealing only with the "visible and tangible side of things." [86] He enunciates this principle: "Although it cannot be denied that science has something to do with truth, it can by no means be accepted as the ultimate measure of truth." Thus, in spite of our unparalleled scientific advance, our age "is perhaps farther away from truth than any previous age." [87] There can be no conflict between science and faith when each stays within its own sphere, but even if one or the other should fail to do so, this very failure means that the conflict is not genuine but sham. Conflict occurs because both science and faith succumb to arrogance and dogmatism. And so, with a strong word of caution about its imperialistic attitude, Brunner salutes science as the means for gaining truth and knowledge about the visible and tangible aspects of the world of our perception.[88]

The truth of philosophy or metaphysics grows out of reflection. It is Brunner's judgment that "the tendency of our age is in this direction." For the philosopher truth is a *Weltanschauung*. This realm of truth lies beyond immediate experience, and it is attained as we discover "the unifying principles of the facts of science and daily experience." This desire to

---

[84] Brunner, *The Theology of Crisis,* pp. 23-24.
[85] Brunner, *Revelation and Reason,* p. 280.
[86] Brunner, *The Theology of Crisis,* p. 23.
[87] *Ibid.*
[88] Brunner, *Revelation and Reason,* pp. 217, 308.

formulate an integrated and comprehensive view of the universe is on a higher plane than the pragmatism and mundane curiosity of the scientist. And yet the shift from scientific to philosophical investigation is not a radical one. In both, man is a "spectator," and he pursues truth "in a cool atmosphere of objectivity and serenity." [89]

Philosophy and faith also stand in close relation and have carried on a great deal of borrowing from one another. Brunner feels, however, that there is "good reason" for the "grave misgivings on both sides" concerning this constant borrowing.[90] The method of philosophy is inadequate for dealing with such religious matters as God, the soul, and ultimate ends, for it employs an aesthetic point of view and is void of passion and lacking in personal decision.[91] Philosophical theories may be used as an escape from reality with its conflicts into "the airy spaces of the sham reality of mere thought." [92] With a strong warning of the danger when it encroaches on faith, Brunner pays tribute to philosophy as the means for developing a theory which gives unity and significance to our experiences.

The truth of faith grows out of passion. This quest for truth "is normal not only to certain men but to man as such." In faith, truth concerns the meaning of existence itself. In this quest for truth, one may well have the objective spirit of the scientist and the universal scope of the philosopher. In science and philosophy, however, one may remain merely a spectator; but not so in faith, for "man himself is in question." Faith is a radically different means of seeking truth because of the passion and involvement concomitant with it. The man of faith seeks truth with the attitude: "I must know or I

[89] Brunner, *The Theology of Crisis,* pp. 24-25.
[90] Brunner, *Revelation and Reason,* p. 375.
[91] Brunner, *The Theology of Crisis,* p. 25.
[92] Brunner, *The Mediator,* p. 596.

shall die"; and Brunner insists: "That is the real search for truth." One cannot concern himself with the relation between God and man, with the source and meaning of his existence, and with all such ultimate questions in a dispassionate way.

The urgency and decisiveness of this question are inseparable from its object; they are correlative to it, so that you may say: "If you do not *so* seek, namely, personally and passionately, you do not seek at all." Your heart will be aflame with the question only when you are dealing with the fiery centre, and not the circumference, of existence.[93]

The other ways of seeking truth are not challenged by faith, but they pale in comparison with it.

It is not merely the way of seeking truth and knowledge that is radically different, but also the nature of the truth that is found and of its effect. The knowledge acquired through faith is so fundamentally different from that acquired through reason that "one hesitates to call it 'knowledge' at all." Brunner discusses three characteristics which exhibit the sharp contrast between the two types of knowledge. First, in rational acquisition of knowledge the knowing subject is master of and superior to each object; but in revelation the knowing subject is a conditioned subject and is mastered by the unconditioned subject. Second, ordinary knowledge enlarges the learner but does not transform him; it enriches but makes no change. In revelation it is exactly the opposite; one is not informed or educated but transformed. Third, natural knowledge is of objects, and so the process of learning is an isolated one; but in faith, to know means to commune, primarily with God and secondarily with one's fellowmen.[94]

In another passage[95] Brunner discusses six characteristics

[93] Brunner, *The Theology of Crisis,* pp. 25-27.
[94] Brunner, *Revelation and Reason,* pp. 26-28; *Truth as Encounter,* pp. 114-18.
[95] Brunner, *Revelation and Reason,* pp. 369-72.

of Christian truth which stand in contrast with those of rational truth. Christian truth happens; it is not truth that "is," i.e., it is not timeless truth. Christian truth is personal or "Thou" truth. Christian truth is given and must be continually received afresh. Christian truth and reality are inseparably combined. Christian truth is a personal encounter which enables one to break through the "ring of immanence" which surrounds him. Christian truth is acquired only through an act of personal surrender. Christian truth and knowledge are fundamentally and radically other than rational knowledge and truth.

When we ask the question, "Just what is Brunner's appraisal of the value of reason?" the trumpet gives an uncertain sound. Each particular note is usually sufficiently clear and distinct, but when you listen to them together there is a strange medley of reveille and taps. With one breath, a clarion call comes to reason; with the next, a dirge falls upon it. At one moment reason is stirred to action; at another, it is laid to rest. But finally one's ear becomes attuned, and it is possible to pick out major and minor themes. The major theme is that reason's day of supremacy is over; the minor theme, that reason is still a valuable servant in those areas where its use is warranted. Brunner is never really concerned with the problem of whether or not to use reason, but rather his concern is to determine reason's "sphere of reference," i.e., where it is to be used and where it is not to be used.[96] Faith is not opposed to reason as such, but only to its unwarranted use. "For the claim of faith does not summon the rational man to suspend his intellectual habit of control and examination of facts; all that faith claims is that he must not try to exercise it in a sphere where it has no function." [97] *Caveat emptor,* however,

[96] *Ibid.,* p. 380.
[97] *Ibid.,* p. 208.

for this statement might not be quite so innocuous as it sounds. It might be balanced by saying that Brunner thinks reason is like the girl in a nursery rhyme of whom it is said: "When she was good, she was very, very good; but when she was bad, she was horrid."

Reason can be used to develop theological thought, but it cannot lead one to the truth with which theology is concerned. Brunner analyzes dogmatics into two elements. It "is not *only* a process of thought *about* that which is given in faith, it is at the same time *believing thinking*." [98] Hence, the theologian's work is not purely rational; yet it cannot be denied that rational thought is a major activity for him. Indeed, it is his rational activity which distinguishes the theologian as such within the believing community. Brunner puts it quite vividly: "For that which differentiates the theologian from the simple old woman who believes in Christ is not his greater faith but his greater power of thought in the service of faith." Hence, Brunner goes on to admit that "there are not merely negative, but also positive, relations between revelation and reason." [99] He will not describe the definition of man as a rational animal as a false definition, but insists that it is certainly inadequate. To understand man correctly we must start not with his rational nature but with his responsibility.[100] It is faith that initiates and sustains theology, but reason may be used to develop it. Brunner compares the process of thinking in theology to a movement resulting from the interaction of two forces which tend in different directions, choosing tangential and centripetal forces for purposes of illustration.

[98] Brunner, *The Christian Doctrine of God*, p. 76.

[99] Brunner, *Revelation and Reason*, p. 16.

[100] *Ibid.*, p. 55. Brunner develops an anthropology based on the understanding of man as responsible to the Word of God in *Man in Revolt* and *The Word of God and Modern Man*, tr. by David Cairns (Richmond, Va.: John Knox, 1964).

The purely rational element of thought, logic, has the tendency to go straight forward from each given point; but faith continually prevents this straightforward movement by its pull towards the Centre. So instead of a movement in a straight line there arises a circular movement around the Centre—and that is a picture of real theological thinking. Theological thinking is a rational movement of thought, whose rational tendency at every point is continually being deflected, checked, or disturbed by faith.[101]

Without reason there is no movement or development of thought; but without faith there is no Christian thought—stagnant or otherwise—and whatever thought there is leads us away from the truth of revelation. In the very act of conquering reason, Christ "makes it free *to serve*." [102] Faith is the *sine qua non;* reason, although a potential enemy of faith, is yet a valuable servant when it acts under the aegis of faith.

Reason can be used to make decisions, but it cannot be the final court of appeal. The logos of reason is to be replaced by the incarnate logos as "the final criterion of valid assertions." [103] The criterion of reason is "abandoned as useless," and this attacks reason at its "central point." [104]

Reason, however, rebels and refuses to recognize any curtailment of its sphere of jurisdiction. To recognize the claim of faith is a humbling experience; so, in the last analysis, human opposition to faith springs from pride rather than reason. Such pride is "the heart of sin," for it is man's assertion of his will to be like God and his denial of God's majesty and sovereignty.[105]

Thus Brunner contends that faith is not really an opponent of reason but of "the irrational arrogance of those who

---

[101] Brunner, *The Christian Doctrine of God,* p. 76.
[102] Brunner, *Revelation and Reason,* p. 430. Italics mine.
[103] Brunner, *The Philosophy of Religion,* p. 16.
[104] Brunner, *The Mediator,* p. 108.
[105] Brunner, *The Theology of Crisis,* pp. 42-43.

pride themselves on their intellect, and of the irrational self-sufficiency of reason." [106] Yet Brunner is aware that he is not asking reason merely to give up its delusions of grandeur. He is not asking reason merely to restrict its activity in territory where it has no just cause to operate, and to carry on business as usual elsewhere. The implications are much more serious than this. "If what the Christian faith says be true, then not only this or that system, but every system, as such, is false; indeed, any faith in a system which—even if only approximately—could be perfected, is false." Both human reason and pure or theoretical reason are "robbed of the predicate of ultimate truth." [107] Reason can continue to make its decisions, but for Brunner these decisions are those of a witness and not of a judge.

In his later writings,[108] Brunner places some stress on the fact that reason is indispensable for the reception of revelation. Although a mystery, revelation is never magic. Although creating a new understanding, revelation passes through and lays claim upon the natural understanding. Revelation addresses man in human speech, words, grammar, and images. "Faith does not speak with celestial tongues, but with the words of ordinary speech." Revealed knowledge and rational knowledge

are as far from each other as heaven is from earth. And yet, in the very act of expressing this sentence, writing it down, and printing it, we have already put in use the whole apparatus of the human reason and of human culture. Whoever forms sentences,

[106] Brunner, *Revelation and Reason*, pp. 16-17. Note Brunner's reference to the irrationality of an arrogant reason. For example, unaided reason may lead to atheism, pantheism, speculative idealism, deism, agnosticism, positivism, or theism *(Ibid.,* pp. 348-61). Each of these claims to be "according to reason" *(Ibid.,* p. 348).

[107] Brunner, *The Mediator,* p. 108.

[108] Brunner, *Revelation and Reason,* pp. 15-16, 416; *The Christian Doctrine of God,* p. 73; *Truth as Encounter,* pp. 100-102.

even if they are sentences full of heavenly wisdom, does so, not only and not primarily, but still in the strength which comes from the fact that he possesses reason; for apart from reason there is only "speaking with tongues"—and perhaps not even this.[109]

Although man is entirely passive in the reception of revelation, still he is totally involved, and "thus revelation does not extinguish the human reason but claims it wholly for this process of reception." Indeed, "revelation presupposes a receptive spiritual subject," and hence it can come only to man, who alone of creation is endowed with reason. Brunner's insistence that reason is necessary for the reception of revelation may have saved reason from exile, but it has hardly restored its dignity and status. Reason is thought of by Brunner much as if it were an indispensable but untrustworthy servant, whom it is impossible to dismiss yet necessary to keep under constant surveillance.

Inadequacy of this Concept of Revelation

In this and the previous chapter we have examined the understanding of revelation and how it yields doctrine according to the encounter theology of Buber and Brunner. Briefly stated, the thesis of encounter theology is that revelation as personal encounter yields doctrines only indirectly. Revelation is encounter with the eternal Thou and is completely free of I-It elements. Doctrine is produced by later rational reflection upon encounter and is not necessary to revelation. Both the Bible and the church point beyond themselves to witness to the possibility of divine-human encounter. Theology is necessary to preserve and protect the church's witness to this availability of the personal presence, and consequently theology is sub-

[109] Brunner, *Revelation and Reason*, p. 16.

ordinate to the church's witness. Theological propositions depend upon, but are never adequate to express, the faith which is prior to them. Trust does not depend upon assent and operates in a different sphere.

For Buber revelation is "the disclosure of the Presence" *(Gilluy ha-Shekinah)* and not "the giving of the Torah" *(Mattan Torah),* which implies propositional content. Buber rejects the orthodox interpretation of the Torah and argues that the Torah does not present truths but the possibility of personal relation to God. Even at Rosenzweig's urging Buber would not make the slightest concession toward a recognition of objective elements in the Torah. Buber insists that knowledge about God is not necessary to encounter. In his own words: "It is not necessary to know something about God in order really to believe in him: many true believers know how to talk to God but not *about* him." Faith is trust in a person *(emunah)* rather than acknowledgment of truth *(pistis).* Knowledge about God comes from reflection upon the encounter, of which knowledge-about is never an adequate expression.

Brunner disagrees with Buber's view that *emunah* and *pistis* are different types of faith. Brunner denies that the Christian belief in doctrines and in historical events necessitates assent rather than trust. He further argues that historical and doctrinal elements are involved in *emunah,* as well as in *pistis.* "Buber's understanding of faith is not identical with that of the Old Testament, but . . . *one* essential element is missing in it. Buber's concept of faith does not make it clear that even Old Testament faith is an answer to God's action in *historical events* and in the prophetic Word." [110] But despite this minor point of disagreement, Buber and Brunner hold essentially the same position.

[110] Brunner, *The Christian Doctrine of the Church, Faith, and the Consummation,* p. 161.

For Brunner revelation is not the reception of truths from or about God but is personal relation with God. The content of revelation is not some*thing* but some*one*, viz. God himself, not ideas about him or from him. Theology is necessarily provisional, since it is the attempt to express by means of words that which cannot be expressed adequately by such means. Theology depends upon faith and is intelligible only to those who already believe.

The basic question that I would like to raise concerns the adequacy of encounter theology's explanation of how revelation yields doctrine. Buber and Brunner contend that revelation is free of I-It elements, and that theological doctrines are exclusively the product of subsequent rational reflection upon encounter. And yet, in practice, this methodological principle is not adhered to strictly.

The usual form of Brunner's concession seems to be the recognition that in spite of being in a different sphere theological truth is not unrelated to, but grows out of, encounter. For example, Brunner must grant that although theology is subordinate and inadequate, it is nevertheless a necessary task. Again, the Bible is granted to involve some degree of doctrinal reflection, though minimal and not theologically systematized. Brunner even talks of a "destructive misunderstanding" of the faith, but such a phrase seems to make sense only if encounter with Jesus the Christ is considered to involve doctrinal interpretation.

At times Brunner seems to make an even stronger concession, although he shows no obvious awareness that he is doing so. He seems to imply that knowledge-about is the essential vehicle of encounter. He says that "faith cannot exist apart from sound doctrine," and that incorrect doctrine does not point man to God, though witness does not depend "exclusively" upon sound doctrine. Brunner recognizes that however minimal our knowledge about the Word of God may be, it is nonetheless true that, in his own words, "we only come to the knowledge of him where definite words and statements about him are made, and expressed, and understood." Brunner differentiates between the personal Presence and doctrine as the framework which bears or conveys the personal Reality, and says that these have a necessary, not accidental, relation to one another. He recognizes "an abysmal difference, and yet at the same time a necessary connection" between revelation and doctrine.

Brunner's failure to develop this latter implication that doctrine is a vehicle of encounter seems to be a major weakness in his understanding of encounter. The distinction between testimony and doctrine, important as it is, becomes overdrawn when it is suggested that testimony has no element of doctrine in it, and ceases to be testimony when it assumes doctrinal form. Brunner seems to overlook the significance of the context of communication and the vital and essential role of interpretation in his insistence that there is a sharp contrast between "Thou art the Christ" (testimony) and "He is the Christ" (doctrine). These statements should not be understood in isolation from a context of communication. If, as Buber insists, the mere vocalizing of the word "Thou" does not establish relation, neither, it would seem, should the vocalizing of the word "he" in and of itself establish the I-It connection.

Buber insists that human encounters point toward their fulfillment in the encounter with God. He contends that we come to God through relations with other persons, not by individualistic renunciation of such relations as Kierkegaard contended. One cannot help but wonder why other persons should cease to point us to God when the I-Thou relation fades into an I-It connection. Buber even grants that we do not come to God through renunciation of objects. But if God encompasses all the spheres in which relation may occur, why can we not say further that I-It objects may serve as means of relation with

God? Buber is quite insistent that relation with God is independent of knowledge about God; yet he will concede that systematic and rational thought is indispensable. "Systems of thought are manifestations of genuine thought-relations to being made possible through abstraction. They are not mere 'aspects,' but rather valid documents of these cogitative voyages of discovery." [111] But if, as both Buber and Brunner concede, systematic and rational thought is indispensable, then I-Thou encounter and I-It doctrine are more integrally related than is expressed in the explanation that the latter is independent of and subsequent to the former.

The inevitability of I-It knowledge for encounter theologians is also seen in their branding of fundamentalist-orthodox theologians as "bibliolaters." To make this accusation it is necessary to employ objective I-It knowledge. The charge of bibliolatry cannot be made in strict consistency with the thesis that doctrine is solely the product of later rational reflection upon encounter. However, encounter theologians have failed to recognize the I-It basis of their doctrine of the Scripture as testimony to, rather than record of, revelation. Let us examine the role of I-It knowledge in the encounter theologians' charge that fundamentalist-orthodox theologians are bibliolaters.

In making the charge of bibliolatry encounter theologians are unaware that they are indebted to the liberal doctrine of the Bible as a fallible human document. Liberal theologians responded to the scientific revolution by distinguishing between scientific and religious truth so that it was possible to accept the scientific world view without destroying or undercutting the significance of the Bible as a book of religion, and as a human product. Because of the work of liberal theologians, encounter theologians can reject the futile efforts of proposi-

[111] Buber, *Eclipse of God*, p. 60.

tional theologians to preserve the infallibility of the Bible. But because it assumes the work of liberalism, it is easy for encounter theology to ignore the fact that its own understanding of the Bible is informed by I-It knowledge and is not a result of the interpretation of faith by later reflection upon divine-human encounter. The Bible is recognized as a fallible, human document because of the influence of scientific (I-It) knowledge.

Brunner is not oblivious to the impact of science and biblical criticism on man's understanding of the Bible,[112] but in general he tends to depreciate the significance of scientific data and to ignore the personal elements in scientific knowledge. Brunner's subordination of the findings of natural science and biblical criticism is clearly expressed in his statement that the error of verbal inspiration

is not so much that its advocates do not see and concede the inaccuracies and human fallibility of the holy Book—that is the argument of the Enlightenment, which is indeed right, but does not touch the central point. The error is that through this (aprioristic) Bible faith, faith has been transformed into something fundamentally different from what the Bible itself means by *pistis* and *emuna*.[113]

Whereas propositional theologians, as we shall later see, have failed to distinguish between scientific and religious questions, encounter theologians have failed to recognize the significance of scientific questions by subordinating them. Brunner says

[112] For example, see Brunner, *Revelation and Reason*, pp. 273-93. For a discussion of the personal element as indispensable to science, see Michael Polanyi, *Personal Knowledge* (Chicago: University of Chicago Press, 1958), and contrast this with Brunner's distinction between the truths of science, philosophy, and faith as described in the previous section.

[113] Brunner, *The Christian Doctrine of the Church, Faith, and the Consummation*, p. 190.

further: "Even the most outstanding scientific discoveries, such as those of Copernicus or Darwin, barely penetrate the surface of man's being. It is through misunderstanding of their real importance that scientific questions arouse any depth of interest. Taken by themselves they have not the 'temperature' of truth." [114] Clearly, for Brunner even science at its best is relatively unimportant.

It is appropriate to distinguish scientific and religious questions, but the relation of faith to science is to foster science and not merely to accept it. Indeed, modern empirical science depends both historically and logically upon Christian as well as upon Greek thought and could not have arisen from the latter tradition alone. It is significant that that which is the main interest of contemporary science was minimized as only "accidental" in Greek thought. For example, Aristotle says quite clearly: "When we tell 'what' a thing is, we do not indicate whether it is white or warm or three cubits long, but that it is (for example) a man or a god." Contemporary science, in contrast with Aristotle, is keenly interested in color (measured in wave lengths), in heat (measured in Centigrade or Fahrenheit), and in length (measured in inches, centimeters, and so forth). It is the Christian understanding of God as Creator that underlies the transition from the description of created reality as "accidental" to its present status as the focal point of scientific investigation. There is a genuine insight, and not merely an expression of piety, in Francis Bacon's two-fold basis for hope in the possibility of a reconstruction of science on a new foundation. His first basis is theological, viz. that the nature of God as the Author of Good and the Father of Lights inspires confidence in the quest for understanding nature; his second basis is methodological, viz. that

[114] Brunner, *The Theology of Crisis*, p. 24.

previous failures are no basis for discouragement because they pursued the wrong road to understanding.[115]

Brunner ignores the creative relationship between science and Christian theology, and he also ignores the contribution of science to his own understanding of the Bible. For with all his subordination of science, Brunner regards the Bible as a human fallible document ultimately on the basis of the impact of scientific data and not on the basis of rational reflection upon encounter. We will later have to examine the defense against the charge of "bibliolatry" and come to some verdict; but at this time it is sufficient to note that the very mention of the charge by encounter theologians implicitly involves I-It elements.

But, if the practice of encounter theology involves I-It elements, we must either emend it or replace it with another theory. Our next task will be to examine the case for propositional revelation and to see whether it can make any contribution to our final position. My contention is that the theory of propositional revelation has something to contribute, although it is not viable in its traditional form and is incapable of emendation. When we have seen that there is no turning back to the theory of propositional revelation, it will then be possible to reconsider encounter theology, proposing an emended form which will provide a satisfactory explanation of how revelation yields doctrine.

---

[115] *Novum Organum,* Book I, aphorisms xciii-xciv. The argument that empirical science depends in part on Christian theology stems from M. B. Foster, "The Christian Doctrine of Creation and the Rise of Modern Science," *Mind,* XLIII, 1934, pp. 446-68, and is developed in John Baillie's *Natural Science and the Spiritual Life* (New York: Scribner's, 1952) and Gilkey's *Maker of Heaven and Earth,* pp. 109-120. However, this thesis is discounted by John Dillenberger, *Protestant Thought and Natural Science* (Garden City, N. Y.: Doubleday, 1960), pp. 16-17.

5. Propositional Revelation

Our investigation now makes a sharp about-face. We turn from the Buber-Brunner tradition of revelation through non-propositional encounter to the concept of propositional revelation as advocated in American fundamentalism and European orthodoxy. We are concerned with the major areas of disagreement between encounter and propositional theology on the problem of how revelation yields doctrine. Consequently, our attention will be directed primarily to the significant points of difference and contrast on this issue rather than to the similarities.

Fundamentalism is represented by J. Gresham Machen and B. B. Warfield, and orthodoxy by Abraham Kuyper. The three men are sufficiently agreed to allow an interweaving of their ideas without distortion. The discussion focuses on the views of inscriptured revelation (Bible), systematized revelation (theology), and on the inadequacy of propositional theology.

Warfield and Machen both taught for more than twenty years at Princeton Theological Seminary. Warfield's tenure of office was from 1887-1921. Machen began in 1906, and when the fundamentalist controversy resulted in an institutional realignment in 1929, he helped organize the conservative Westminster Theological Seminary where he taught until his death in 1937.[1] Our discussion of the Machen-Warfield tradition of American fundamentalism will be supplemented by reference to the work of Kuyper, a Dutch theologian and politician whose main concern was to revivify a conservative form of Calvinistic theology. In their English translation both of Kuyper's major works have an introduction by Warfield.[2] These three men represent the era of classic formulation of the theory of propositional revelation, a point of view which encounter theology consciously avoided in its own reaction to liberal theology. It is for this reason that these men are basic to our discussion. Contemporary conservatives advocate essentially the same position as that of Machen, Warfield, and Kuyper, but most are more irenic in spirit, more appreciative of other kinds of theology, and more aware of the social responsibilities of Christianity.[3]

We will also look at some contemporary attempts to emend the tradition of Machen, Warfield, and Kuyper. This procedure will enable us to consider propositional theology in terms of

[1] Machen chafes under the label "fundamentalist." He laments: "For the life of me I cannot see why adherents of the Christian religion, which has been in the world for some nineteen hundred years, should suddenly be made an '-ism,' and be called by some strange new name" (J. Gresham Machen, *What Is Christianity?* ed. by Ned Bernard Stonehouse [Grand Rapids, Mich.: William B. Eerdmans, 1951], p. 134). Machen insists that the position which he holds is in the central current of Christian life and in historic continuity with the early church *(Ibid.,* p. 253.)

[2] Abraham Kuyper, *Principles of Sacred Theology,* tr. by J. Hendrik de Vries (Grand Rapids, Mich.: William B. Eerdmans, 1954); *The Work of the Holy Spirit,* tr. by Hendrik de Vries (New York: Funk & Wagnalls, 1900).

[3] Cf. Arnold W. Hearn, "Fundamentalist Renascence," *Christian Century,* April 30, 1958, p. 528 and Carl F. H. Henry, *Evangelical Responsibility in Contemporary Theology* (Grand Rapids, Mich.: William B. Eerdman's, 1957), especially chap. two.

its classical, formative period (with footnote references to parallel discussions in contemporary writings) and also in terms of attempts to appropriate this position for the contemporary period.

Inscriptured Revelation

The relation of the Bible to revelation is a basic area of disagreement between propositional and encounter theologians, and it can be contended that other differences are but logical outgrowths of this major divergence. God reveals himself through propositions which are recorded in the Bible. These are then systematized into doctrines and assent to them is the basis of appropriating the revelation through faith in Jesus Christ.

NATURE OF THE BIBLE

There is a sharp contrast between propositional and encounter theology on the nature of the Bible. Both emphasize the uniqueness of the Bible, but from this point the views diverge. For propositional theology the Bible is an "open" revelation, in the sense that it is complete in and of itself for the entire race. Kuyper draws this analogy: "Public charity may provide each poor man a sum of money with which to buy provisions for himself, or may spread in a hall a common table from which all poor people may be fed." [4] Kuyper rejects the opinion that God has chosen the former method and insists that we are given in the Bible a complete and open revelation.

As an "open" (objective) revelation, the Bible is subject to

[4] Kuyper, *Principles of Sacred Theology*, p. 360. Cf. B. B. Warfield, *Counterfeit Miracles* (New York: Scribner's, 1918), p. 26.

investigation and verification. Warfield asserts that the superior lucidity of the written revelation establishes it as the norm of interpretation for all other methods of revelation.[5]

It is interesting to compare Buber's attack on the mystic for emptying one of the bearers of relation with Warfield's charge that the mystic takes his religious experience as his authority, instead of taking the Scripture as his norm and interpreting and guiding his religious experience in its light.[6] Both Buber and Warfield are critical of the subjectivism of the mystic, but for different reasons. Buber criticizes the mystic for withdrawing from personal relation; Warfield, for withdrawing from an objective norm.

For propositional theology the Bible provides an objective Word of God. This view does not agree with the contention of encounter theology that revelation is not of truths but of a personal presence. The value of the written form of revelation is that it provides objectivity. However, Kuyper does point out that writing serves merely an auxiliary function and would not be necessary if our powers of memory and our capacity for communication were not limited. But because of these limitations it was necessary that the self-revelation of God assume a written form. The written word, as contrasted with the spoken word, has the qualities of durability, catholicity, fixedness, and purity.[7] The apostles not only gave the church

[5] B. B. Warfield, *Studies in Theology* (New York: Oxford University, Press, 1932), pp. 61-63.

[6] *Ibid.*, pp. 649-66, especially pp. 654-55, 658-59. For Machen on mysticism see J. Gresham Machen, *The Christian Faith in the Modern World* (Grand Rapids, Mich.: William B. Eerdmans, 1947), pp. 117-20. Cf. also R. A. Finlayson, "Contemporary Ideas of Inspiration," in *Revelation and the Bible,* ed. by Carl F. H. Henry (Grand Rapids, Mich.: Baker Book House, 1958), pp. 228-30.

[7] Kuyper, *Principles of Sacred Theology,* pp. 405-12. Cf. Martin, "Special Revelation as Objective," in Henry, *Revelation and the Bible,* pp. 63-64, who speaks of preciseness, accuracy, and range as the values of language and of permanency as the value of writing. In connection with the latter he points out that a written will is preferable to an oral.

of their day a fixed form of life, for which purpose their spoken word was sufficient, but they also provided a means of preserving the pure teaching of the church through the ages and propogating it throughout the world by preparing a written documentation of the revelation given through Jesus Christ. Hence Kuyper asserts that the epistolary activity of the apostles, or more specifically, "the objectifying of Christian truth in the apostolic epistles is the most important of all their labors." [8] By assuming written form revelation becomes objectified and open for all.

Encounter theologians consider the Bible to point beyond itself to the possibility of revelation, but propositional theologians contend that revelation can be found within the Bible. Machen specifically rejects the view that the Bible *contains* the Word of God and insists that it *is* the Word of God.[9] Indeed, he insists that "all that we can know" of supernatural revelation "is found in the pages of one Book." [10] It is conceivable to Machen that we might discover information about supernatural revelation given in Bible times but not recorded in the Bible, but he discounts the possibility. He concludes: "On the whole, speaking broadly, we can certainly say that all the supernatural revelation that we can be at all certain about, although no doubt other supernatural revelation was given in Bible times, is recorded in the pages of one book, the Bible." [11] However, the qualifying phrases that open this sentence, the inclusion of the phrase, "that we can be at all certain about," and the admission that other supernatural revelation was undoubtedly given loosen the boards of Machen's otherwise

[8] Kuyper, *The Work of the Holy Spirit,* pp. 146-49.

[9] J. Gresham Machen, *The Christian View of Man* (Grand Rapids, Mich.: William B. Eerdmans, 1947), p. 2; *The Christian Faith in the Modern World,* pp. 56-58. Cf. Ned B. Stonehouse, "Special Revelation as Scriptural," and Finlayson, "Contemporary Ideas of Inspiration," in Henry, *Revelation and the Bible,* pp. 75-76, 230-34.

[10] Machen, *The Christian Faith in the Modern World,* p. 29.

[11] *Ibid.,* p. 33.

tightly built structure. Moreover, Machen indicates that the biblical accounts, because they relate events which we must experience as spectators rather than participants, are not sufficient to satisfy our personal desire for revelation.[12] In other words, they are secondhand; they are not the revelation itself, but the record of it. Machen is cognizant of the distinction between revelation and the record of revelation, and also of the fact that this opens up the questions of the adequacy and accuracy of the record and of the degree of certainty with which we can approach it.[13] This leads us to our next consideration, the authority of the Bible.

BIBLICAL INFALLIBILITY

The question of the authority of the Bible is raised by the distinction between the belief that the Bible is the record of revelation and the belief that it is the witness to revelation. The issue is basically a question of the extent, if any, to which the record of the revelation is fallible. Whereas Brunner understands the Bible as a human, and therefore fallible, testimony to revelation, propositional theology contends that the Bible, when properly understood, is a source of absolutely trustworthy knowledge of God.[14] Warfield insists that the method and content of one's theology hinges on this issue,[15]

[12] J. Gresham Machen, *Christianity and Liberalism* (Grand Rapids, Mich.: William B. Eerdmans, 1946), pp. 40-44.

[13] Machen, *The Christian Faith in the Modern World,* pp. 31, 33-34.

[14] Cf. Finlayson, "Contemporary Ideas of Inspiration," in Henry, *Revelation and the Bible,* pp. 225-28. Cf. also Packer, who insists that modern study has not *proved* the fallibility of the Scripture but has *assumed* it as a working hypothesis and has proceeded to interpret Scripture accordingly (James I. Packer, "Contemporary Views of Revelation," in *Ibid.,* p. 96). Cf. pp. 103-4.

[15] Warfield, *Studies in Theology,* p. 99; *The Inspiration and Authority of the Bible,* ed. by Samuel G. Craig (Nutley, N. J.: The Presbyterian and Reformed Publishing Co., 1948), pp. 120-21. Cf. Packer, "Contemporary Views of Revelation," in Henry, *Revelation and the Bible,* p. 89.

and even if this is an overstatement, the nature of the authority of the Bible is undoubtedly a crucial, and therefore hard-fought, issue.

Let us attempt to clarify further the issue that has been raised by this discussion before we proceed to examine the means by which propositional theology considers the biblical record to have been protected from human fallibility. There is no debate as to whether or not God employed human agency in the writing of the Bible. The debate is over the effect that this has had on the resultant product. Warfield's position is reflected in this statement concerning the New Testament writers.

It would be inexact to say that they recognize a human element in Scripture: they do not parcel Scripture out assigning portions of it, or elements in it, respectively to God and man. In their view the whole of Scripture in all its parts and in all its elements, down to the least minutiae, in form of expression as well as in substance of teaching, is from God; but the whole of it has been given by God through the instrumentality of men.[16]

Warfield's emphasis is not on the reception of revelation but on its source.

Since revealed religion must be imposed on man from without by a "source superior to his own spirit," it has an authority which is lacking in natural religions, which "flow from no higher source than the human spirit itself." Warfield's principle is stated axiomatically: "Authority is the correlate of revelation, and wherever revelation is—and only where revelation is—is there authority." [17] Similarly, Kuyper argues that if the Bible is a human link in the chain of God's special revelation, then we must critically evaluate it to see which portions are dependable. But in doing this we have annulled the special

[16] B. B. Warfield, *Biblical Foundations* (Grand Rapids, Mich.: William B. Eerdmans, 1958), p. 62.
[17] Warfield, *Studies in Theology,* p. 650.

revelation and reduced it to natural revelation.[18] After a study of the term *"theopneustos,"* Warfield concludes that the origin of the Bible is to be found in the activity of God in the Holy Spirit as opposed to an activity of man.[19] But even so, human activity is involved in the process, and the ultimate origin of the Bible in God's self-revelatory activity is not sufficient to establish the infallibility of the biblical record of revelation.

VERBAL INSPIRATION

The infallibility of the biblical record is supported by adding the doctrine of verbal inspiration to the doctrine of revelation. We have considered Brunner's attack on the doctrine of verbal inspiration in the preceding chapter. Now let us examine the propositional theologians' understanding of this doctrine. Revelation and inspiration are distinguished by Warfield on the basis that the former refers to the communication of truth and the latter to its recording.[20] However, the intimate relationship between the two is brought out in this statement: "Revelation is but half revelation unless it be infallibly communicated; it is but half communicated unless it be infallibly recorded." [21] Similarly, Kuyper suggests that just as ice is organically one with coldness, so the content of God's revelation is organically one with its form, i.e., the Bible. One cannot perceive ice apart from the cold nor can one apprehend

---

[18] Kuyper, *Principles of Sacred Theology,* p. 362. Cf. J. Theodore Mueller, "The Holy Spirit and the Scriptures," in Henry, *Revelation and the Bible,* pp. 272-73.

[19] Warfield, *The Inspiration and Authority of the Bible,* p. 296. Cf. J. I. Packer, *"Fundamentalism" and the Word of God* (Grand Rapids, Mich.: William B. Eerdmans, 1958), pp. 77, 85-89.

[20] Warfield, *The Inspiration and Authority of the Bible,* p. 421. Cf. Finlayson, "Contemporary Ideas of Inspiration," in Henry, *Revelation and the Bible,* pp. 222-23. However, Stibbs contends that inspiration is primarily applicable to the writings rather than to the writers ("The Witness of Scripture to its Inspiration," in *Ibid.,* pp. 107-8).

[21] Warfield, *The Inspiration and Authority of the Bible,* p. 442.

knowledge of God apart from an infallible Bible. Nonetheless, it is important that the distinction be made as a preventive against the intellectualist error that the Bible alone is sufficient to constitute real revelation.[22] Inspiration in the general sense must not be confused with inspiration of the Bible, since much that was spoken and written under inspiration is not recorded in the Bible.[23]

The inspiration of the Bible is considered to be supernatural, in the sense that it is unique and not to be confused with other types of inspiration; that it is extraordinary, in that it is an action of the Spirit beyond the normal activity involved in conversion and sanctification; and that it produces an absolutely infallible and authoritative report.[24] For Warfield the Bible is an "oracular book," in the sense that in *every* place it speaks as the Word of God.[25] It does not contain man's report or version of what God says but a direct communication.

Not a Word of God that speaks to us only through the medium of our fellow-men, men of like passions and weaknesses with ourselves, so that we have to feel our way back to God's word through the church, through tradition, or through the apostles, standing between us and God; but a Word of God in which God speaks directly to each of our souls . . . through human lips and pens.[26]

There has been an attitude of "entire trust in every word of the Scriptures" throughout the history of the church.[27]

[22] Kuyper, *Principles of Sacred Theology,* pp. 362-63.
[23] *Ibid.,* pp. 504-8.
[24] Warfield, *The Inspiration and Authority of the Bible,* p. 420; Machen, *The Christian View of Man,* pp. 3-4; *Christianity and Liberalism,* pp. 72-73. Cf. Packer, *"Fundamentalism" and the Word of God,* pp. 79-82, 94-101.
[25] Warfield, *The Inspiration and Authority of the Bible,* pp. 106-7.
[26] *Ibid.,* pp. 124-25.
[27] *Ibid.,* pp. 105 ff. Cf. pp. 169 ff. Cf. Packer, "Contemporary Views of Revelation," Geoffrey W. Bromiley, "The Church Doctrine of Inspiration," Finlayson, "Contemporary Ideas of Revelation," Everett F. Harrison, "The Phenomena of Scripture," and Gaebelein, "The Unity of the Bible," in Henry, *Revelation and the Bible,* pp. 103-4, 204-17, 232-34, 237-39, 395.

It is strongly asserted, however, that the inspiration and guidance of the Holy Spirit in no way violated the individuality of the biblical writers, making them perform as mere machines.[28] Machen argues that to espouse a mechanical theory is to impoverish the meaning of "verbal inspiration" by making it apply only to the words and not to the writers themselves.[29] He insists that God prepared men by heredity and environment to write spontaneously that which he wished to communicate.[30] Such a view is obviously based heavily on the Calvinistic understanding of the sovereignty of God and his complete ordering of all events.

The verbal or plenary inspiration of the Bible is affirmed only for the original copy, or autograph, and not for translations, nor even for scribal copies.[31] Indeed, Machen would not hold that any one of the multitude of Greek and Hebrew manuscripts is free from error. "Every one of the manuscripts contains errors; no one of them is perfect." It would seem that Machen has conceded a great deal. Perhaps it is an awareness that he has done so that prompts him to go to great pains to point out that the errors are not significant, and that, although God did not work a miracle to transmit and translate the Bible, still he did so order the lives of his creatures that we do not have to base our assurance on the efforts and results of textual

[28] Machen, *The Christian Faith in the Modern World*, pp. 46-47; *Christianity and Liberalism*, pp. 73-74. Cf. Packer, "Contemporary Views of Revelation," Finlayson, "Contemporary Ideas of Inspiration," Gaebelein, "The Unity of the Bible," in Henry, *Revelation and the Bible*, pp. 95, 223, 395-96, and Packer, *"Fundamentalism" and the Word of God*, pp. 78-79, 178-79.

[29] Machen, *The Christian Faith in the Modern World*, pp. 47-53.

[30] *Ibid.*, pp. 36-37, 45, 59; Warfield, *Biblical Foundations*, pp. 67-72; Kuyper, *Principles of Sacred Theology*, pp. 513-17. Cf. Packer, *"Fundamentalism" and the Word of God*, p. 78.

[31] Machen, *The Christian Faith in the Modern World*, pp. 38-39. Cf., however, the additional assertion that the presence of the living Spirit "pervades the translated Word as truly as the original text" (Finlayson, "Contemporary Ideas of Inspiration," in Henry, *Revelation and the Bible*, p. 224).

scholarship.[32] Despite Machen's assurances, many readers may wonder why such loud and forceful protestations of full and complete accuracy are forthcoming for autographs which no longer exist. And the concession that the records with which we must deal may contain inaccuracies, however slight, does seem to involve Machen in subjective evaluation of the biblical record.

In light of these comments, it will be interesting to consider what Machen and Warfield have to say about the importance of affirming plenary inspiration. Machen insists that this doctrine "belongs not to the superstructure but to the foundation. If a man really holds to it, everything else for that man is changed." [33]

Even so, Machen does distinguish between those who reject the doctrine of plenary inspiration but are still Christians, and liberals, "who reject the supernatural acts of God with which Christianity stands or falls." Even though the former do not believe that the biblical writers were supernaturally guided and do believe that the Bible contains many errors, they are still within the Christian framework because they believe that the Bible is right, at the central point, in its account of the redeeming work of Christ.[34] Similarly, Warfield will concede that the foundations of the faith are not dependent upon the doctrine of plenary inspiration, or upon any doctrine of inspiration.[35] Indeed, not only could there be Christianity without an infallibly inspired Bible, but there could even be Christianity

[32] Machen, *The Christian Faith in the Modern World*, pp. 39-44. Cf. p. 54. Also cf. Packer, *"Fundamentalism" and the Word of God*, pp. 90-91; Finlayson, "Contemporary Ideas of Inspiration," and Harrison, "The Phenomena of Scripture" in Henry, *Revelation and the Bible*, pp. 231-32, 239-40. For a discussion of the findings of textual criticism, see also Nic. H. Ridderbos, "Reversals of Old Testament Criticism," and Merrill C. Tenney, "Reversals of New Testament Criticism," in *Ibid.*, pp. 335-50, 353-67.

[33] *Ibid.*, p. 37.

[34] Machen, *Christianity and Liberalism*, pp. 75-76.

[35] Warfield, *The Inspiration and Authority of the Bible*, p. 121.

without any Bible whatsoever. However, Warfield seems appalled by the mental image of this theoretical possibility, and he intones: "But to what uncertainties and doubts would we be the prey!—to what errors, constantly begetting worse errors, exposed!—to what refuges, all of them refuges of lies, driven!" [36] And so, with Machen and Warfield, the doctrine of plenary inspiration may not be the *esse* of Christianity, but it most assuredly is necessary for its *bene esse*.

ANSWER TO BIBLIOLATRY CHARGE

Since we have considered Brunner's charge that propositional theology is guilty of bibliolatry, let us now consider the case for the defense. [37] The defense may be presented in terms of three basic assertions: (1) the Bible is recognized to be temporary; (2) the Bible is recognized to be incomplete without the supplementation of the inner witness of the Spirit; and (3) the paper and ink is recognized as important only insofar as it conveys the divine message. The assertion that the Bible serves as a testimony to Christ might also be considered as a line of defense, but it is not so considered here because of the propositional theologians' extreme insistence on the inviolability of the record. The record itself, although it testifies to Christ, seems to do so because of its impeccability, and thus appears to become sacrosanct. Thus the argument of its testimony to Christ is dependent on the basic assertions that will be considered here.

The first argument of the defense is that special revelation is abnormal and temporary. Kuyper grants that special revelation is both richer than and a necessary supplement to natural theology, but he further insists that "this does not take away

[36] *Ibid.*, p. 442.
[37] Cf. Packer, "Contemporary Views of Revelation," Finlayson, "Contemporary Ideas of Inspiration," and Gaebelein, "The Unity of the Bible," in Henry, *Revelation and the Bible*, pp. 96, 232, 400-401.

the fact that natural theology always remains the originally real one, and that special revelation can never be anything else than accidental." [38] Special revelation is but an adaptation to our human situation. It is analogous to the necessity of communicating with a deaf person with some substitute for sound, such as lipreading.[39] Kuyper employs several illustrations to point out the abnormal and temporary nature of special revelation. He likens natural theology to legs and special revelation to crutches which have become necessary because of an abnormal condition of the legs.[40] Special revelation is also likened to a bandage or to intravenous feeding, which may be necessary to save life but which is an artificial and temporary expedient. Choosing another sphere for illustration Kuyper compares special revelation to a scaffold, which may even hide the house, and which may remain in position for a long time, but which is destined to be removed eventually.[41]

If man enjoyed immediate communion with God the Bible would be a hindrance, interposing itself between God and man. Accordingly, the Bible will cease to be of value to us upon our death. But we do not now enjoy face to face communion with God, and so in our present condition the Bible is not a hindrance but a necessity. The Bible is likened to artificial light which may be turned off when the sun shines in the house but which is of tremendous value when the sun has set. Kuyper argues that the Bible is not his idol but an abnormal and temporary expedient.[42]

[38] Kuyper, *Principles of Sacred Theology*, p. 308. Cf. pp. 358-59, 416-19. Cf. the insistence that although general and special revelation must be distinguished, they must also be considered as harmonious (G. C. Berkouwer, "General and Special Divine Revelation," in Henry, *Revelation and the Bible,* pp. 13-24).

[39] *Ibid.,* p. 379. Cf. *The Work of the Holy Spirit,* pp. 61-64, 72.

[40] *Ibid.,* pp. 309-10.

[41] *Ibid.,* pp. 389-90.

[42] *Ibid.,* p. 371; *The Work of the Holy Spirit,* p. 60; and Abraham Kuyper, *Calvinism* (Grand Rapids, Mich.: William B. Eerdmans, 1943), pp. 54-57.

The second line of defense is that the Bible is not idolized since it is considered incomplete without the inner testimony of the Holy Spirit. This testimony is "absolutely indispensable" because the Bible does not convey knowledge of God mechanically so that everyone who reads it thereby gains a true knowledge of God. The Holy Spirit not only gave the Scriptures but he remains "the perpetual author *(auctor perpetuus)* of all appropriation of their contents *by* and of all application *to* the individual." "The Word of God" does not refer to the Bible as a printed book, but to the Bible as the agency or means of operation for the Spirit of God within man. Even the most glittering diamond is as dull as any piece of carbon if rays of light are not entering it. Likewise, the beauty and power of the Bible are due to the fact that the Holy Spirit may shine through it, and without this concomitant it is a dull and inert book. It is not, propositional theology insists, the Bible as a book that is worshiped, but the God who shines through this book by the power of his Spirit.[43]

On the surface this position sounds simliar to that of Buber and Brunner. However, there is a basic difference. For Buber and Brunner the Bible is not a source of knowledge about God but is a potential means through which God may be encountered. For propositional theology, the Spirit, among other things, convinces one of the truth of the knowledge about God contained in the Bible. The agreement of propositional and encounter theologians *that* the inert written word must be vitalized by the inner activity of the Spirit should not blind us to the more important disagreement as to *how* the written

[43] Kuyper, *Principles of Sacred Theology*, pp. 360, 298, 401-2, 555. The inner testimony of the Spirit receives a much stronger emphasis in propositional theology than is often supposed, e.g., see Packer, "Contemporary Views of Revelation," Bromiley, "The Church Doctrine of Inspiration," Finlayson, "Contemporary Ideas of Inspiration," Mueller, "The Holy Spirit and the Scriptures," Gaebelein, "The Unity of the Bible," in Henry, *Revelation and the Bible*, pp. 95, 216, 224, 267-81, 398-400, and Packer, *"Fundamentalism" and the Word of God*, pp. 110-13.

word becomes vitalized. For the encounter theologian the word becomes vitalized when it serves as a channel through which the reader establishes personal relation with God; for propositional theology it becomes vitalized when the reader feels an inner conviction that the words he is reading are true and are the words of God.

The third line of defense is that the charge of bibliolatry is based on a misconception of the nature of books in general and the Bible in particular. To those who object that a book is dead and lifeless, Kuyper replies that they do not know what a book is. "A book is not merely paper printed in ink, but is like a portrait—a collection of lines and features in which we see the likeness of a person." The words printed with ink on the pages of the Bible, far from being its essence, "are but tokens of recognition; those words are only the clicks of the telegraph-key signaling thoughts to our spirits along the lines of our visual and auditory nerves." [44] No book is to be thought of merely as marks of ink on paper. But more is to be said than this.

The Bible is unique among books. To begin with, it is "neither a lawbook nor a catechism, but the documentation of a part of *human life,* and in that human life of a *divine process.*" [45] The Bible is not an independent entity, linking man and God, but is rather the medium by which God becomes directly present to man.[46] The source of the Bible is not man but God. This is highly significant because life and thought are inseparable in God, whereas the unity of life and thought has been severed in man. "Hence our cold abstractions; our speaking without doing; our words without power; our thoughts without working; our books that, like plants cut off from their

[44] Kuyper, *The Work of the Holy Spirit,* pp. 56-57.
[45] Kuyper, *Principles of Sacred Theology,* p. 377. Cf. pp. 413-14, 419, 564-66.
[46] *Ibid.,* pp. 58-59, 65, 347-48, 364.

roots, wither before they can blossom, much less bear fruit." [47] Kuyper says that if the Bible were a human book, partaking of the falsehood that has entered human hearts and has severed word and life and placed them in opposition, then he would agree with those who exalt life above the Word. But he insists that this is not necessary since the Bible, being the work of God, was not thus affected.[48] Let us close the defense with this eloquent plea from Machen:

Let it not be said that dependence upon a book is a dead or artificial thing. The Reformation of the sixteenth century was founded upon the authority of the Bible, yet it set the world aflame. Dependence upon a word of man would be slavish, but dependence upon God's word is life. Dark and gloomy would be the world, if we were left to our own devices, and had no blessed Word of God. The Bible, to the Christian, is not a burdensome law, but the very Magna Charta of Christian liberty.[49]

This is a strong case for the defense; but is it strong enough? In a moment we shall have to render a verdict. But first let us examine how propositional theology employs the Bible as the source book of theological doctrines.

Systematized Revelation

For the fundamentalist-orthodox tradition theology is the systematized form of the propositions which are infallibly revealed in the Bible. This is the second major area of contrast between propositional and encounter theology in their understanding of how revelation yields doctrine. Our task here is to understand how propositional theology understands the necessity of theology, the Bible as the source book of theology, and the objective nature of theology.

[47] Kuyper, *The Work of the Holy Spirit,* p. 57.
[48] *Ibid.*
[49] Machen, *Christianity and Liberalism,* pp. 78-79.

Necessity of Theology

Both encounter and propositional theologians consider theology a necessary task but differ in the reasons assigned. According to encounter theologians, witness, not doctrine, is primary, and theology is necessary to protect the church's message from destructive misunderstanding, and to provide a norm for the church's preaching. Theology is not an individual undertaking but is carried on within the context of the witness of the church and of the Holy Spirit. Propositional theologians are also concerned with such witness, but for them there is no witness, whether by the church or the Holy Spirit, apart from doctrine. Because doctrine is not subordinate to but essential to witness, theology is a theoretical discipline grounded in the individual, rather than a practical discipline grounded in the church.

In this vein Warfield insists that revelation is "the correlate of understanding and has as its proximate end just the production of knowledge, though not, of course, knowledge for its own sake, but for the sake of salvation." [50] According to Warfield the chief factor which distinguishes man from animals is man's direction of his life by intelligence, and therefore theology is based on reason.

However, this is not a thoroughgoing individualism, for intelligence not only distinguishes man from animal but also binds man to man. Kuyper says: "There is a world of thought which binds man to man, and which, notwithstanding the change of individuals, passes on from generation to generation." Although only a few men feel at home in this world of thought, all men "derive general representations from this world of thought which are the common property of all and thereby render the mutual correspondence among minds possible." The knowledge of God is no exception to the pervasive

[50] Warfield, *Biblical Foundations,* p. 20.

influence of this element of human life, and theology "is born from the thirst after insight and clearness, and cannot rest so long as there is still a possibility of making the insight into its object more clear." [51]

The human intellect necessarily systematizes, whether well or ill, the facts it grasps, and if we had as few as two facts about God, the intellect would contemplate them in relation to one another.[52] The very nature of man as an intelligent being necessitates theological activity as a primary concern of the individual.

SOURCE BOOK OF THEOLOGY

Encounter theologians would agree that man's reason is involved in the reception of revelation, but the contrast with propositional theology comes out clearly in the disagreement over the amount of theological reflection found in the Bible. For Brunner, it is present but minimal. Since for propositional theology the Bible does not merely contain but is the Word of God, and since the Word of God was given in propositional form, the Bible is a collection of loci for the use of the theologian. For Machen, the New Testament, even its earliest documents, is "radically doctrinal." [53] Warfield says: "All the facts given to us by Scripture are given as 'dogma.' " [54]

In accord with human nature, God's self-revelation is given in terms of knowledge which can be grasped by man's intelligence.[55] Jesus Christ and the prophets and apostles not only related the series of Christian facts but also their correct in-

[51] Kuyper, *Principles of Sacred Theology*, pp. 328-30.
[52] Warfield, *Studies in Theology*, p. 95.
[53] Machen, *What Is Christianity?*, pp. 153, 277-79.
[54] B. B. Warfield, *The Right of Systematic Theology (Edinburgh:* T. & T. Clark, 1897), pp. 42-43.
[55] Warfield, *Biblical Foundations*, p. 21; Machen, *What Is Christianity?*, p. 254.

terpretation.[56] The mighty acts of God become revelatory by virtue of producing knowledge of God and of his purpose.

No bare series of unexplained acts can be thought . . . adapted to produce knowledge, especially if these acts be, as in this case, of a highly transcendental character. Nor can this particular series of acts be thought to have as its main design the production of knowledge; its main design is rather to save man.[57]

The mighty acts of God must be not only narrated but also explained. It should be emphasized that the explanation of the mighty acts of God is not simply added to the narration but is integrally related to it. Indeed, it is so vitally connected that the explanation itself must be considered one of the mighty acts of God.[58] The deeds are not revelatory without the explanatory word, for without doctrine the facts would have no meaning or significance for us.[59] "What Christianity consists in is facts that are doctrines, and doctrines that are facts. . . . Its facts and doctrines entirely coalesce. All its facts are doctrines and all its doctrines are facts." [60] From the beginning the church has proclaimed its gospel in terms of both an event and its meaning. " 'Christ died'—that is history; 'Christ died

---

[56] Warfield, *The Right of Systematic Theology*, pp. 39-40, 61; *Studies in Theology*, pp. 41-43; Machen, *Christianity and Liberalism*, pp. 31-33. Cf. Jewett, "Special Revelation as Historical and Personal," in Henry, *Revelation and the Bible*, pp. 55-56.

[57] Warfield, *Biblical Foundations*, p. 20.

[58] *Ibid.*, pp. 20-21; *Studies in Theology*, p. 42. Cf. Packer, *"Fundamentalism" and the Word of God*, pp. 91-94. N. B. "the biblical position is that the mighty acts of God are not revelation to man at all, except insofar as they are accompanied by words of God to explain them" *(Ibid.*, p. 92).

[59] Warfield, *Studies in Theology*, pp. 41-42; *The Right of Systematic Theology*, p. 35. Cf. Jewett, "Special Revelation as Historical and Personal," Stonehouse, "Special Revelation as Scriptural," Packer, "Contemporary Views of Revelation," and Finlayson, "Contemporary Ideas of Inspiration," in Henry, *Revelation and the Bible*, pp. 48-52, 83-84, 100-102, 221-220. Packer says that "the idea that revelation, imperfectly mirrored in the Bible, is directly available in the historical events of which the Bible bears witness . . . somewhat suggests a divine charade, to be solved by the God-inspired guesswork of human spectators" *(Ibid.*, p. 100).

[60] Warfield, *The Right of Systematic Theology*, p. 34.

for our sins'—that is doctrine. Without these two elements, joined in *an absolutely indissoluble union,* there is no Christianity." [61] Facts and doctrines are not merely necessary components of the gospel; they are essential to one another.

According to Machen, systematic theology, as well as biblical theology, may be based on the Bible, since the Bible contains not merely doctrines but a system of theology.[62] And yet great effort is needed to extract that system. As Kuyper points out,[63] the Bible is not written in the form of a notarized report or a legal code, in which case any statement which literally and fully expressed an assertion could be considered authoritative and final without reference to context. The task of the theologian is much more complex than simply compiling proof texts. He must first determine the meaning of the biblical writers; then he must assimilate the content thus discovered into his own consciousness, putting it into categories and into a synthesis meaningful to himself; and finally he must reproduce this in the form of a confession or witness. By this means he studies the Bible as recorded revelation, but it must also be studied in its interaction with the life and work of the church. Consequently, the history of the church must also be studied as an integral task of theology. But this does not alter the basic stance of propositional theologians toward the Bible as a source book of theology. As Warfield states it: "The Holy Scriptures are the source of theology in not only a degree, but also a sense in which nothing else is." [64]

[61] Machen, *Christianity and Liberalism,* p. 27. Italics mine. Cf. p. 29; *What Is Faith?,* pp. 149-51.

[62] Machen, *What Is Christianity?,* pp. 145, 229, 277-78.

[63] Kuyper, *Principles of Sacred Theology,* pp. 564-78. Cf. Gaebelein's view that although the Bible is "the primary source book of Christian doctrine," nonetheless "the Bible is much too living a book for its unity to be centered in doctrinal formulation, however vital and dynamic the doctrines are" ("The Unity of the Bible," in Henry, *Revelation and the Bible,* pp. 391-92).

[64] Warfield, *Studies in Theology,* p. 63.

What role does human interpretation play in the use of the Bible? For Machen, that depends on what is meant by the question. He will agree that interpretation is a factor if we mean that each race and generation can make its own contribution "to the rich store of our understanding of what God has told us in His Word." But Machen suspects that what is implied by the question is that the interpretation of each race and generation is valid for itself alone. He rejects this theory on the basis that it involves the danger of substituting the race's or generation's imagination for contact with the real person, Jesus of Nazareth, "whom God has presented to all nations in the whole of His Word, not only in the four Gospels, but also, just as truly, in the Epistles of Paul." Human interpretation of the Bible is, for Machen, influential only on one's own understanding and in no way limits or affects the written record on which the interpretation is based.[65]

NATURE OF THEOLOGY

Since the Bible is the source book of theology for propositional theology, there is no such subordination of the role of reason as is found in encounter theology. Whereas Buber and Brunner contrast the objectivity and detachment of science with the involvement and commitment of faith, the propositional theologians describe theology as "the science of God." They mean by this that theology proceeds by intellectually systematizing revealed facts about God. There is no distinction of levels or types of truth and knowledge, and no contrast between the knowledge of faith and of reason.

According to Machen, theology analyzes and systematizes the facts on which Christianity is based. Hence he makes the claim that in spite of wide differences in subject matter and

[65] Machen, *What Is Christianity?*, pp. 30-31. Indeed, no generation will be able to complete this task. Cf. Warfield, *Studies in Theology*, p. 76; Kuyper, *Principles of Sacred Theology*, pp. 402, 567.

in qualifications required of the investigator, theology is just as much a science as any of the natural sciences, such as chemistry, for both are concerned with the acquisition and systematization of a body of truth.[66]

Though it may seem like a strong statement, Machen's plea for equality is, as a matter of fact, quite a step-down from Warfield's position. Warfield contends that since theology is an inductive study of facts conveyed in a written revelation, it has an advantage over all other sciences which must undertake an inductive study of facts which are conveyed in life and which are consequently much more difficult to interpret.[67] And with this assertion, any seeming innocuousness of the statement that theology is a science should be effectively dispelled. Warfield considers it imperative to defend two principles: "the principle of a systematized body of doctrines as the matter to be believed, and the principle of an external authority as the basis of belief." [68] Warfield insists that a doctrinal element lies at the very base of Christianity.[69] From its very inception Christianity has "ever come to man as the rational religion, making its appeal primarily to the intellect." [70]

The task of theology is expressed by Kuyper in the phrase "logical action." [71] Logical action is that action by which man "of himself and of necessity" transposes the "content in his heart to *knowledge of God,* in the form of thought and word."

[66] J. Gresham Machen, *What Is Faith?* (New York: Macmillan, 1925), pp. 32, 231-42; *Christianity and Liberalism,* p. 19; *What Is Christianity?,* p. 255. Cf. Kuyper, *Principles of Sacred Theology,* pp. 290, 567.

[67] Warfield, *Studies in Theology,* p. 74. Warfield lists three prerequisites of any science: "(1) the reality of its subject-matter; (2) the capacity of the human mind to apprehend, receive into itself, and rationalize this subject-matter; and (3) some medium of communication by which the subject-matter is brought before the mind and presented to it for apprehension" *(Ibid.,* p. 53). See pp. 55-56 for an expanded version of the same three presuppositions or prerequisites.

[68] Warfield, *Studies in Theology,* p. 587. Cf. p. 585.

[69] Warfield, *The Right of Systematic Theology,* p. 61.

[70] *Ibid.,* p. 89.

[71] Kuyper, *Principles of Sacred Theology,* pp. 268-75, 299.

Buber is willing to abandon objective assurance and to rely rather on the personal assurance gained through encounter with God. For Kuyper, however, the personal relationship to God consists of nothing more than a bundle of perceptions, impressions, and feelings, and one must employ logical action to advance from this to knowledge of God and transform revelation into theology. The reason that knowledge of God was not revealed to us in dialectical, discursive form, but in veiled, symbolic form, is "in order that it might be valid for every age and people, for every time of life, grade of development, and condition." [72] As a result, the propositional theologian sees his task as difficult and arduous, but he would not agree with Brunner that theology is merely an intellectual abstraction.

Yet we must be careful to notice that for propositional theologians the science of theology in no way increases knowledge of God. Rather, it gives a clearer insight into the revealed knowledge of God and makes a fuller assimilation of its contents possible. Kuyper employs this illustration: "The microscope adds nothing to the wing of the butterfly, but enables me to obtain a richer knowledge of that wing." In another illustration he says that although the church owes not a single pearl of her confession to theology, "it is equally certain that she would not have been able to string these pearls so beautifully in her confession had not the light of theology illumined her spiritual labor." Theology adds nothing to the knowledge of God but rather increases man's ability to apprehend it.[73]

Underlying the view that theology enables us to apprehend knowledge of God is the view that revelation is objective. Propositional theologians will grant the incompleteness of our knowledge of God and the limitations of our intellect, but they refuse to abandon the position that our knowledge is true and

[72] *Ibid.,* p. 295.
[73] *Ibid.,* pp. 292, 329.

our intellects reliable as far as they go.[74] Buber contends that revelation is transitory, in the sense of not enduring beyond the moment of divine-human encounter. In sharp contrast with this point of view, propositional theology considers revelation to produce a content which is objectively there for man to grasp or apprehend.

Because of the necessity of human apprehension of theological truths, propositional theologians consider theology a "progressive science," but we must note clearly what they intend and do not intend by this phrase. A sharp distinction is drawn between the progress of a science and an increase in its material.[75] From the beginning the church possessed complete knowledge, and no subsequent development will enable it to surpass the apostles, although this does not preclude the idea of development through history in the understanding of the truth.[76] Kuyper compares the Bible to a gold mine, which is complete and can never have anything added to it, but which can be explored by succeeding generation, although the Bible, of course, is not quiescent and passive like the gold mine, but rather exerts a dynamic power through the working of the Holy Spirit.[77] He also uses the illustration of the progress of medical science in the understanding of herbs, although no new herbs are produced, nor are new medicinal qualities contributed to them.[78] Warfield expressed this view succinctly: "The affirmation that theology has been a progressive science is no more, then, than to assert that it is a science that has had a history." [79]

[74] *Ibid.*, pp. 290, 567; Machen, *What Is Faith?*, pp. 27, 32-33, 51-52, 66, 152-53; *What Is Christianity?*, p. 255.
[75] Warfield, *Studies in Theology*, p. 75.
[76] Kuyper, *The Work of the Holy Spirit*, pp. 164-65.
[77] *Ibid.*, p. 165; *Principles of Sacred Theology*, p. 573.
[78] Kuyper, *The Work of the Holy Spirit*, p. 166.
[79] Warfield, *Studies in Theology*, p. 75.

The Failure of Propositional Theology

Having noticed some difficulties with the theoretical basis of encounter theology, we turned our attention to propositional theology. We are now in a position to evaluate it as a possible option to encounter theology. The position advanced here is that propositional theology fails to provide an option for the understanding of how revelation yields doctrine. However, this does not mean that propositional theology is completely irrelevant to our problem. Having argued that it does not provide a basis for an adequate understanding of how revelation yields doctrine, we will nonetheless turn, in the next chapter, to an examination of the contribution which propositional theology can make to an emendation of the position of encounter theology.

Verdict on the Charge of Bibliolatry

There is no debate over the importance and centrality of the Bible. Both propositional and encounter theologians agree with John 5:39 that the Scriptures are they which testify of Christ, but they differ as to *how* the Scriptures thus testify. Propositional theologians insist that the function of the Bible in revelation is to serve as its written *record*. Encounter theologians insist that the Bible is to serve as the written *testimony* to revelation. In other words, propositional theologians claim that the Bible *is* the Word of God; encounter theologians, that the Bible *contains* the Word of God. Propositional theologians insist that the Bible is itself revelation; encounter theologians, that the Bible serves as the basis on which revelation is possible.

We have discussed Brunner's accusation that propositional theologians are guilty of both confusing the Bible (as a book) with revelation (as a relationship between God and man) and also of worshiping the Bible in their insistence on verbal inspiration. We have also examined their denial of these charges. Let us now attempt an evaluation of this controversy.

We may grant propositional theologians an acquittal on the first charge, viz. that of confusing the Bible with revelation. They are not guilty of this charge because they recognize the Bible as the objective *record* and *product* of special revelation and not the revelation itself, and they also insist that the Bible serves as a testimony to, not a substitute for, Christ.

However, the second and more serious charge of bibliolatry remains. Here the case is not so easily defended as propositional theology assumes. But neither is it so easily settled as encounter theology assumes. Let us consider the charge and the defense. The encounter theologian contends that the propositional theologian deifies an aspect of creation and is therefore guilty of idolatry. The propositional theologian defends himself by pointing out that he recognizes the Bible to be temporary, to be incomplete without the supplementary testimony of the Holy Spirit, and to be more than paper and ink, and more than a human book. Both accuser and accused assume their case. *If* the Bible is a fallible human creation, then the propositional theologian may be guilty of bibliolatry. On the other hand, *if* the Bible is not a human book but a supernatural creation, then he is no more guilty of bibliolatry than the encounter theologian is of Christolatry. The *de jure* question is easily decided only after we settle the more difficult *de facto* question, and it is this latter question which both propositional and encounter theologians tend to take for granted. Is the Bible a divine-infallible record of revelation or a human-fallible witness to revelation? If the infallibility of the Bible cannot be maintained, then propositional theology cannot escape the verdict of guilty of bibliolatry.

140

THE FATAL CHALLENGE OF SCIENCE

The propositional theologians' assertion of a divine-infallible record of revelation is the reaction to a challenge. It was not until biblical literalism was challenged that it became a fundamental for some theologians. The traditional understanding of the universe and of man's status within it, an understanding which is mirrored in the Bible, came to be radically challenged by the discoveries of science. The Bible pictures man as living on an earth which is the center of God's creation, and from which he will eventually ascend to a spatial heaven or descend to a spatial hell. The literal acceptance of this picture was challenged by the heliocentric theory of Copernicus and further challenged by the work of Kepler, Galileo, and Newton. According to calculations based on "internal biblical evidence," creation was believed to have taken place by divine fiat in 4,004 B.C. The literal acceptance of this manner and time of creation was challenged by such developments as Laplace's elaboration of the nebular hypothesis and Lyell's studies in geology. But not only was the traditional understanding of the universe revolutionized, but also man's role within it was questioned. The most traumatic and vigorously resisted of all the scientific reorientations was that posed by Charles Darwin, whose theory of natural selection raised serious questions about the very nature of man.

Nor was the scientific challenge restricted to the natural sciences, but rather it overflowed into every field of study. For example, if man as an organism had evolved, then it seemed logical to assume that man's ideas and his economic and social institutions had also developed through an evolutionary process. The application of this theory resulted, among other things, in the critical study of historical documents. When the tools of criticism were applied to a study of the Bible, they revolutionized our understanding of the purpose and composition of the biblical writings. There were found to be not only human errors and contradictions in transcription but also such human elements as divergences of theology and purpose in the composition of the books. For example, there is a divergence between the nationalism of Ezra and Nehemiah and the universalism of Jonah and Ruth. Even the biblical picture of Jesus Christ was seen to be colored by human interests. The Gospels were recognized to be interpretive portraits rather than factually accurate narratives.

It was in reaction to the challenges of natural science and historical criticism that some theologians not merely accepted the statements of the Bible literally but established the theory of the verbal infallibility of the Bible as the foundation of their theology. Even so, the propositional theologians, making greater concessions than they realized, accepted lower, or textual, criticism and claimed infallibility only for the autograph or original copy. Brunner notes that acceptance of textual criticism opens the door to a "searching" criticism of the present text. He remarks that since "the divergence of this original text from the present text must be considerable, if the critical observations on the present text were to be satisfied, there came into being an infallible Bible-X, of which two things only were known: first, that it was the infallible word of God; and, secondly, that although it was very different from the present one, yet it was still the same Bible." [80] Unlike the biblical critics' hypothetical "Q," the "Bible-X" of propositional theology is not a heuristic assumption productive of further understanding, but is a purely apologetic measure, devised to defend the doctrine of verbal infallibility. But can the theory of verbal infallibility be successfully defended?

Ironically, the propositional theologians did not emphasize verbal infallibility until this theory was no longer tenable. The

[80] Brunner, *Revelation and Reason,* pp. 274-75.

literal nature of the statements in the Bible had been assumed prior to the scientific revolution, but this assumption had never been made the basis of a theological system. After the scientific revolution a system based on such an assumption was doomed to failure. Certainly the death was not immediate but is protracted, and there are individuals and areas in which belief in verbal infallibility continues to flourish. But the doctrine of infallibility is nonetheless doomed to succumb. Why is this? A clue is found in John Baillie's remark that discussion of the relation between science and religion

is constantly vitiated, and the complexity of it unduly simplified, by its being thought of as a relation between the outlooks of two different men. . . . Surely the depth of the problem emerges only when the man of science and the man of faith . . . are but two elements in the total outlook of a single mind.[81]

It is obvious that religious faith and acceptance of scientific data coexist in a person, but Baillie's reminder is salutary because we tend to overlook this in the process of analysis. We all enjoy the benefits of science, such as automobiles and television sets. Our enjoyment of these things is lengthened by such scientific products as vaccines and surgical procedures, the pain of which is greatly reduced by anesthesia. Even our worship is conducted in sanctuaries which are dependent on science for electrical illumination. Science is pervasive in our lives, and any theology which is contradicted by it is doomed to eventual failure since the theology must coexist with the person's scientific perspective.

There is increasing awareness among propositional theologians that they must achieve some sort of rapprochement with science. They cannot follow the lead of liberal theology in understanding the Bible as a book of religion rather than a

[81] *Natural Science and the Spiritual Life,* p. 6.

book of science, and as a human-fallible rather than divine-infallible book. Yet they want to live with the modern, scientific world view but still retain the theory of biblical infallibility. Can this be accomplished? Let us consider two efforts.

Although Packer does not abandon infallibility, he is critical of nineteenth century fundamentalism. He finds greatest fault with its ventures into natural science. "Here, where the fundamentalists' confidence was greatest, their competence was least, and their performance brought ridicule and discredit on themselves." [82] Packer argues, however, that God is author both of Scripture and of nature, and that there can be no conflict between science and the Bible if they are rightly understood. "We shall, therefore, continue loyal to the evidence both of Scripture and of empirical inquiry, resolved to do justice to all the facts from both sources while we wait for further light as to the right method of relating them together." [83] But right understanding of the Bible involves a careful understanding of what is and is not meant by the term "infallibility."

Infallibility means that God has spoken in the Bible, which is therefore absolutely true, reliable, and authoritative. Since the Bible makes no claim to be a textbook of science, its infallibility does not make it normative for modern science. Nor does infallibility of the Bible mean that any interpretation of it is infallible.[84] Before evaluating this effort of Packer's, let us consider a similar position.

Ramm is also critical of the strategy of nineteenth-century fundamentalism, without rejecting its basic approach. He points out that the early fundamentalists had little time to formulate a strategy, and that until recently university training was primarily literary and classical rather than scientific,

[82] Packer, *"Fundamentalism" and the Word of God*, p. 32.
[83] *Ibid.*, p. 135.
[84] *Ibid.*, pp. 95-98.

so that the nineteenth-century fundamentalists had to work with little awareness of the relevant scientific data.[85] Ramm feels that only superficial attention has been given to the nature of biblical language concerning natural things. He considers it important to understand that the language of the Bible concerning natural things is popular (not technical), prescientific (but not anti-scientific), and nonpostulational (i.e., free of theorizing as to the actual nature of things).[86] Ramm holds firmly to the propositional theologians' principle of the infallibility of the Bible even on scientific matters.[87] He attempts to reconcile the Bible and modern science by distinguishing between inspiration and interpretation. "Revelation is the communication of divine truth; interpretation is the effort to understand it." [88] Consequently, agreement on the inspiration and divine origin of Genesis 1, for example, does not necessitate agreement on its interpretation. There is a wide variety of possible interpretations of the six days of creation, each of which is tenable without sacrificing belief in biblical infallibility.[89] Ramm, like Packer, makes a distinction between the Bible as interpreted by men and the Bible as infallibly revealed by God.

The argument of propositional theology as elaborated by Packer and Ramm in the light of modern science is commendable for the integrity and quality of its scholarship. And

[85] Bernard Ramm, *The Christian View of Science and Scripture* (Grand Rapids, Mich.: William B. Eerdmans, 1954), p. 21.

[86] *Ibid.*, pp. 65-80.

[87] *Ibid.*, pp. 25, 32-33, 39. Insisting that only propositional revelation can be revelation of truth, Ramm considers propositional revelation one of the criteria for distinguishing between theology that adheres to, and theology that repudiates, historic Christianity. His argument focuses on the affirmation: "There must be a conceptual or a propositional element in revelation or otherwise revelation is no more the Word of God as truth" ("The Continental Divide in Contemporary Theology," *Christianity Today*, Oct. 8, 1965, p. 15).

[88] *Ibid.*, p. 40. Cf. pp. 40-42.

[89] *Ibid.*, pp. 173-229.

yet, far from buttressing the theory of biblical infallibility, it is actually a concession to science. They insist on an infallible Bible, but because of the influence of science on their own *Weltanschauung* they are saying in effect: "The Bible is infallible in what it actually says, but we have to look to science to determine whether an interpretation is a possible expression of what the Bible really says." With this kind of argument propositional theology is not preserving the infallibility of the Bible vis-à-vis science, but rather has turned the Bible into a weak echo of what science says with greater precision and force.

Propositional theology is not the only position to manifest irony in its relation to science. We have noted in an earlier chapter that encounter theology subordinates science yet relies on it for its understanding of the Bible as a fallible-human document. Liberal theology, which encouraged a high regard for science, tended to make a Kantian dichotomy between science (dealing with the "is") and religion (dealing with the "ought"), so it brought science and religion together by assigning them to separate spheres. The situation is ironical indeed! Propositional theology attacks science, but follows it; encounter theology ignores science, but accepts it; liberal theology befriends science, but keeps it at a distance.

The distinction between revelation and interpretation not only fails to preserve the Bible inviolate from the advances of modern science; it also renders the concept of infallibility insignificant. If the Bible must be interpreted by men, and if any human interpretation is fallible, what difference does it make whether that which is being interpreted is itself infallible, and how could we possibly determine this? Not only is the "Bible-X" far separated from us by the process of transcription and translation but also by the process of interpretation. Even if we had an infallible autograph in our possession we would have to interpret it fallibly.

THE IMPOSSIBILITY OF SUCCESSFUL EMENDATION

Is it possible, then, to emend propositional theology by responding to the impact of science with an acknowledgment of scientific fallibility, but without surrendering infallibility on religious issues? Could we contend that the Bible is fallible on matters of science and history, but nonetheless infallible as a source book of doctrine?

Even if infallibility were claimed only for doctrinal issues, propositional theology would flounder at the point of the necessity of interpretation. Perhaps an illustration will be helpful.

Let us assume that Mr. White finds in the Bible the proposition, "Jesus Christ is the Son of God." Mr. White says that since it speaks of Jesus Christ as the Son of God, he must be inferior in status and a creation of God. Mr. Black, on the other hand, says that the eternal Father must have an eternal Son, and therefore the proposition means that Jesus the Christ and God the Father are coequal and co-eternal. Without entering the debate, let us merely ask what significance we can find in the assertion that the proposition "Jesus Christ is the Son of God" has been supernaturally guarded so that it is verbally infallible? It seems to have no practical significance whatsoever. Even though verbal inspiration may be a theoretical possibility, there is still no infallibility because the proposition must be interpreted. To interpret the meaning of a proposition we must go beyond the words to fathom the purpose of the speaker, and this opens the door for distortion—less widely in science, more widely in religion, but it is always ajar.[90] The fundamentalist-orthodox

[90] Cf. the view that "language behavior is purposive behavior" in Abraham Kaplan, "Philosophic Sense and Mystic Sensibility," *Proceedings and Addresses of the American Philosophical Association,* XXXII, October, 1959, p. 44.

insistence on an infallibly inspired Bible is based on a false view of propositions as independent of any context of communication.

Roman Catholicism may also be considered as presenting an alternative effort to establish infallibility. Does it provide any clues for a possible emendation of propositional theology? Roman Catholics recognize the necessity of interpretation but claim an authoritative interpretation on the basis of natural theology and the role of the church as preserver and interpreter of the faith once delivered to the saints. Theoretically, natural theology is a rational and objective standard to which all men can appeal, but in practice it has not been sufficiently convincing to settle disputes. Moreover, the whole enterprise of natural theology has fallen into disrepute as an inappropriate method of gaining religious knowledge, since it distorts God into an object of human investigation and research. The appeal to the role of the church as preserver and interpreter of the tradition does not solve the problem either, although it does posit a living authority to which one can resort.[91] But even if the church provides an infallible interpretation of the Bible, it cannot guarantee that this will be infallibly communicated. Mr. White and Mr. Black may differ in their understanding of what the church means by its teaching, just as they differed in their understanding of what the Bible means by its teaching.

Another possibility is to assert infallibility of something other than propositions. This would no longer be propositional theology, but it could certainly be a possible emendation of propositional theology. An example of this kind of attempt is found in Austin M. Farrer's *The Glass of Vision*

[91] Brunner argues that in practice, though not in theory, the authority of the church to interpret Scripture serves to eliminate the function of the Scripture "as a critical court of appeal" *(The Christian Doctrine of God,* pp. 44-45).

(1948) and *A Rebirth of Images* (1949). Granting the force of the argument against the theory of divinely revealed propositions, Farrer counters with the theory of divinely revealed images. His stress on the significance and creative power of imagination is in many ways a pleasant change from the more arid rationalism of propositional theology. Indeed, most forms of theology have tended to neglect the imaginative powers of man in favor of the intellectual powers. But does Farrer's theory enable us to escape the dilemma that confronts propositional theology? There is nothing about images that makes them capable of infallible impartation, and if anything, they would seem to be more vulnerable to varying human interpretation than are propositions.

It seems that any emendation of propositional theology inevitably undercuts the principle of biblical infallibility, which the emendation is supposed to safeguard by locating fallibility in human interpretation rather than in the Bible itself. If interpretation is fallible, there is no significance in an infallible record of revelation. And even if an interpretation could be considered infallible, there is no guarantee that the understanding of the interpretation will be infallible. Propositional theology not only fails to provide an adequate understanding of revelation but also it is not capable of emendation. Hence, propositional theology is not adequate as an explanation of how revelation yields doctrine, and we must return to encounter theology to see if it is possible to develop a satisfactory modification of that basic position. Consequently, our task is now to examine propositional theology for whatever help it can provide in dealing with this problem, and then to undertake an emendation of encounter theology that will provide an adequate understanding of how revelation yields doctrine.

6. The Non Sequitur of Propositional Theology

Thus far we have seen that we do not have an adequate explanation of how revelation yields doctrine, either from encounter theology with its insistence that propositional elements are always subsequent to revelation as encounter, or from propositional theology with its insistence that propositions are revealed. In short, encounter theology does not go far enough in its understanding of the role of propositional elements in revelation, and propositional theology goes too far. It would seem, then, that what is needed is an explanation which includes propositional elements within encounter, without going to the extreme of affirming that propositions are revealed.

Before we move to our final statement of how revelation yields doctrine, we must delve even further into the dynamics of the propositional tradition to consider some of the implications of the theory of propositional revelation. The point at which the propositional element is involved most significantly in the process of revelation is in the appropriation of revelation by the response of faith. It is at this point that propositional theology has an enduring contribution to make to our final solution. As a preliminary step toward the construction of a more adequate explanation of how revelation yields doctrine, we shall examine the understanding of faith in propositional theology. Indeed, I would suggest that the preservation of a propositional element in our response of faith is what is of most value in this tradition, and that the theory of propositional revelation is a well-intentioned, but untenable, effort to preserve the dimension of assent to truth as a part of our trust in God's revelation of himself.

Three basic questions will occupy our attention in this chapter. First, is propositional theology necessarily dogmatic? If revealed truths claim our assent, what attitude must we take toward those who differ from us in our understanding of the truth revealed by God? Second, is propositional theology necessarily legalistic? If propositions are revealed, must we not conduct our lives in obedience to their demands? Third, is faith as assent to propositional truth compatible with faith as trust in a person? It is in seeing how propositional theology responds to these questions that we are enabled to discern the essential value of this tradition and the non sequitur which renders its final formulation unacceptable. This non sequitur is basically a jump from the necessity of recognizing propositional knowledge in the process of revelation to description of this element as the infallibly imparted content of revelation. We have already found that the concept of infallibility leads propositional theology into a dead end. It is now our task to see whether it leads necessarily to dogmatism, legalism, and to the exclusion of trust from the concept of faith as intellectual assent to propositions.

The Problems of Dogmatism and Legalism

The insistence of propositional theology upon the objective nature of theological propositions and the infallibility of revelation raises the problem of dogmatism and the appropriate attitude toward an alternative theology. Brunner allows for a relatively wide degree of theological variation. He defines orthodoxy (literally "right doctrine") as rightly directed or rightly oriented doctrine. In other words, the test of doctrine is not where it stands but where it points. Propositional theology, on the other hand, seeks to set forth the facts or truths upon which Christianity is based, and consequently orthodoxy is rightly situated, as opposed to rightly pointed, doctrine. How is one to consider alternative theologies? In general, the answer of propositional theology is that since theology deals with truth, any alternative theology must be considered inferior; but since our knowledge of theology is incomplete, our judgment of other views must be moderated accordingly. Let us examine both elements of this answer.

In spite of its incompleteness, there is an absolute character to theology. This is due to its connection with its object (i.e., God), and it "excludes not only doubt, but also the dilution of subjectivism, as if our formulated statement of the knowledge of God in our confession were unimportant, and *without loss of truth* could be exchanged for every other confession or placed on a line with it." [1] Machen declares that God has given us in the Bible "not merely theology, but a system of theology, a great logically consistent body of truth," which he then proceeds to identify with the Reformed or Calvinistic faith. Other evengelical systems of theology are referred to as "approximations to that body of truth." [2] Machen seems to believe that the incompleteness of theology is of minor significance. A similar mood of almost unbelievable confidence comes out strongly in these two statements by Warfield. Theology, because based on written revelation, not on life, was

[1] Kuyper, *Principles of Sacred Theology*, pp. 254-55.
[2] Machen, *What Is Christianity?*, p. 229.

the first-born of the sciences. It was the first to reach relative completeness. And it is today in a state far nearer perfection than any other science.

However nearly completed our realization of the body of truth may seem to us to be; however certain it is that the great outlines are already securely laid and most of the details soundly discovered and arranged; no one will assert that every detail is as yet perfected.[3]

And so, although these men grant that theology is incomplete, they consider the major points and outlines to be so assured that one can and must brand any alternative theology as inferior or false.

Machen answers two questions that are often prompted by such a rigid point of view. First, is the man who lives a life like that of Jesus not a Christian merely because he does not accept doctrines concerning Christ's redemptive work? Machen replies that our lives are not like that of Jesus, that we are sinners, and that we must be brought into right relation with God through the redeeming work of Jesus.[4] Second, if salvation is by faith in Jesus Christ, how strong does the faith have to be? Machen's answer here is that there are varying degrees of faith, and that God can use even weak faith to accomplish his works, even the work of redemption. Basic to his argument is the statement: "Faith is not a force that does something, but it is a channel by which something is received."[5]

And yet the recognition of the incomplete nature of theology does have some moderating influence on the judgments and actions of propositional theologians. For example, Machen considers it impossible for any man to determine the minimal

[3] Warfield, *Studies in Theology*, pp. 74, 76.
[4] Machen, *What Is Christianity?*, p. 259; *What Is Faith?*, pp. 110-11.
[5] Machen, *What Is Faith?*, pp. 243-51.

doctrinal requirements for being a Christian. The church may set up requirements for church membership, and Machen advocates a much more rigorous application of this procedure than is currently practiced, but he also insists that in the final analysis all such inquiries must be regarded as very rough and entirely provisional.[6]

Moreover, not all points of doctrine are of equal importance. For example, Machen considers the premillennialists guilty of "serious error" but not of "deadly error." Another example is the difference of opinion concerning the mode of efficacy of the sacraments. Machen adjudges this a serious matter but feels that it is better to be wrong about it than to consider it a trifling matter, so that indifference is judged more harshly than error. Other examples discussed by Machen are apostolic succession, Arminianism, and Roman Catholicism. In each case Machen declares that the differences of opinion, although serious, do not prevent him from having fellowship with their adherents. Even in the case of liberals (and it is the thesis of *Christianity and Liberalism* that liberals have abandoned Christianity) Machen says that there need not be any personal animosity between himself and them.[7]

Kuyper expresses the same mood and attitude in terms of a rejection of both the "skeptical" point of view, which fails to evaluate the relative worth of different theological systems, and also the "absolute" point of view, which discards every system of theology but its own as worthless, not merely inferior. The skeptical view destroys the integrity, and the absolute view the unity, of theological conviction.[8] In order to maintain the conviction of the truth of his own system, the propositional theologian must consider any alternative theology inferior, but ideally this critical evalution should

---

[6] *Ibid.*, pp. 155-59.
[7] Machen, *Christianity and Liberalism,* pp. 48-52.
[8] Kuyper, *Principles of Sacred Theology,* pp. 320-27.

include an appreciation for whatever merit the other system may possess.

Machen makes a suprising rebuttal to the liberal's charge of narrowmindedness by turning the charge back on the liberal. Proponents of the view that doctrine is the necessarily changing expression of religious experience, and ought not therefore to be a cause of division of Christians, are accused by Machen of being "guilty of a really astonishing narrowness of mind." The basis of this charge is that such a person

has simply begged the whole question, and has shown that he has never given himself any trouble to understand the other man's point of view. Of course if doctrine is merely the necessarily changing expression of experience, then the whole debate is ended; but it is ended not by a compromise but a complete victory for the Modernist and complete relinquishment by us of everything that we hold most dear.[9]

It is not the man who attacks Machen's view in order to defend an opposing view whom he considers to be narrow-minded. Rather, the narrow-minded man is one who combats a view without attempting to understand it, on the basis that peace is more important than doctrine.[10]

In view of the avowedly dogmatic attitude of propositional theology, and the claim of encounter theologians that this leads to legalism, let us consider the relationship between theology and legalism from the former's point of view. This is closely related to their understanding of themselves as "intellectualist" and "dogmatist." According to Warfield the theologian becomes an intellectualist in the sense that "he recognizes that Christianity is truth as well as life, and as such addresses itself to the intelligence of men, and has

[9] Machen, *What Is Christianity?*, p. 107. Cf. *Christianity and Liberalism*, pp. 2, 161-62; Packer, *"Fundamentalism" and The Word of God*, pp. 41-46, 72-74, 170-71.
[10] Machen, *What Is Christianity?*, p. 107.

claims upon their belief as well as upon their obedience." He becomes a dogmatist in the sense that "he recognizes the objective validity of a body of religious truth upon the attention of all alike as the condition of their religious life." [11]

Encounter theology asserts that theology is subordinate to faith and is intelligible only to those who already believe. The propositional theologian could agree with elements of this view, but basically, in contrast with encounter theology, he asserts the primacy of doctrine over life. Warfield grants that Christianity is a way of life but denies that Christianity consists wholly in life, and not at all in doctrine. He says that he could concur heartily with the principle of the primacy of life over doctrine if it merely meant that only the Christian can understand Christian truth and state Christian doctrine or that doctrine alone cannot produce life. But since it means that the Christian life blooms and flourishes independently of doctrine, Warfield is staunchly opposed.[12] Similarly, Machen describes the conviction that life springs from doctrine as "the very center and core of our faith." [13]

The issue then, for propositional theology, is not whether or not Christianity is a way of life, but rather by what means the Christian life is produced. For Machen, the means by which the Christian life is produced is the rehearsal of facts and their theological interpretation. He parodies his opponents' view by saying that many of them might have expected the first Christian missionaries to go around saying, "We have been living in contact with a wonderful person, Jesus; contact with him has changed our lives; and we call upon you our hearers, without asking puzzling questions, without settling the meaning of his death, without asking

---

[11] Warfield, *The Right of Systematic Theology,* p. 25.

[12] *Ibid.,* pp. 62-65, 83-85.

[13] Machen, *What Is Christianity?,* p. 107. Cf. p. 255; *The Christian Faith in the Modern World,* pp. 88-104.

whether he rose from the dead, simply to submit yourselves to the contagion of that wonderful personality." [14] On the contrary, Machen argues, an historical investigation of early Christianity clearly indicates that it was based solidly upon doctrine.[15]

However, it should be made clear that Machen is contending for the logical, not causal, primacy of doctrine.[16] For Warfield and Kuyper also it is not doctrine that quickens but God who quickens by using doctrine as an instrument by which to complete his work in human life.[17] Machen insists that vital contact with Jesus Christ is not possible if we neglect doctrine, for it is not his person but his message which makes him ours.[18] Even in the Sermon on the Mount, for example, we cannot simply obey the teachings of Jesus, for they are based on doctrine, especially concerning the nature and authority of Jesus Christ, which we must believe prior to our obedience.[19] In response to the question, "What do the Scriptures principally teach?" Machen approves the order of the answer in the Shorter Catechism, "The Scriptures principally teach what man is to believe concerning God and what duty God requires of man," since this answer bases morality upon truth and life upon doctrine.[20]

[14] Machen, *What Is Christianity?*, p. 21.
[15] Machen, *Christianity and Liberalism*, pp. 19-39. Cf. Packer, *"Fundamentalism" and the Word of God*, pp. 42-43.
[16] *Ibid.*, p. 23 n; *What Is Christianity?*, p. 277.
[17] Warfield, *The Right of Systematic Theology*, pp. 84-85; Kuyper, *The Work of the Holy Spirit*, p. 68.
[18] Machen, *Christianity and Liberalism*, pp. 42-44.
[19] Machen, *The Christian Faith in the Modern World*, pp. 160-73. Cf. pp. 179, 188; *What Is Faith?*, pp. 110-13. It is interesting to note in the debate between Wrede and the Ritschlians that Paul knew much more about the details of the life of Jesus than Wrede supposed. But Machen is convinced that the Ritschlians utterly failed to refute Wrede at the central point, viz. that the center of Paul's religious life is found in just those doctrinal elements which the Ritschlians had rejected or minimized as temporary expressions of the redemptive experience *(What Is Christianity?*, pp. 46-49).
[20] Machen, *The Christian Faith in the Modern World*, p. 88.

Warfield contends that doctrine is primary not just in the Christian religion but in all religions. His argument is that all religions have common elements based on the religious nature of man, and that what distinguishes one religion from another are the concepts or doctrines which are peculiar to each religion. It is not life or religious experience which comes first and produces doctrine, but rather doctrine precedes life and is the source of that which is distinctive in each religion.[21] Doctrine is logically prior to religious experience, because, whether formulated or not, doctrine is the instrument through which the religious life is born and nourished.

Because of their understanding of doctrine as instrumental to life, propositional theologians see no incompatibility between a strong emphasis on doctrine and vital Christian experience. Indeed, for them true doctrine, far from being potentially detrimental, is in fact necessary to ethical vitality. They find examples of this relationship in the Bible, both in the Old and in the New Testaments. Let us consider some examples. The Ten Commandments follow the assertion "I am the Lord your God, who brought you out of the land of Egypt, out of the house of bondage" (Ex. 20:2 RSV); and the law of love in Deuteronomy is based on the Shema (Deut. 6:4). Likewise, in the New Testament, the practical or ethical portions of the epistles "are always based upon the great doctrinal passages that precede them; and the ethical demands of Jesus are always based upon his presentation of the facts not only about God but about his own person and about heaven and hell." [22] Following a description of the early church as radically doctrinal and intolerant, Machen describes it as radically ethical, to the extent of considering any profession of faith to be nothing but sham if it permits

[21] Warfield, *The Right of Systematic Theology,* pp. 80-83.
[22] Machen, *What Is Christianity?,* p. 196.

a man to continue in sin.[23] He attributes the power and vitality of the early church to its doctrinal emphasis. He claims that there is "not a trace of any nondoctrinal preaching that possessed one bit of power" in the days of the early Christian Church.[24] And so he not only rejects the charge that a strongly dogmatic religion becomes legalistic and ethically insipid but considers dogmatism necessary to vitality.

This does not mean, however, that propositional theology believes that doctrine in and of itself insures life and vitality. Rather, doctrine is but the instrument through which God works in human life. Indeed, apart from the working of the Spirit of God "there has never been, and never will be, one spark of life produced by all the doctrines in the world." [25] Hence, the insistence on the doctrinal basis of Christianity does not mean that as long as a man's doctrine is sound his conduct is of little importance. Quite the contrary, the espousal of correct doctrine compounds the sin of unethical conduct. "If our doctrine be true and our lives be wrong, how terrible is our sin! For then we have brought despite upon the truth itself." [26]

The answer to legalism is not to remove the doctrinal basis of Christianity. Machen insists that in the modern opposition to doctrine it is not just shallow and arid doctrines that are rejected but the very doctrinal basis of Christianity. Machen insists that lack of doctrinal clarity will undermine the witness of the church and rob it of strength, resulting eventually in despair and spiritual death.[27] Warfield classifies as "deficients" some, though not all, theologians who find propositional truth

[23] *Ibid.*, p. 280. Cf. *Christianity and Liberalism*, pp. 47-48.
[24] Machen, *What Is Christianity?*, p. 279.
[25] Warfield, *The Right of Systematic Theology*, pp. 84-85.
[26] Machen, *Christianity and Liberalism*, p. 48.
[27] *Ibid.*, pp. 45-47; *The Christian Faith in the Modern World*, pp. 136-37; *What Is Christianity?*, p. 124.

distasteful and who consider theology detrimental to religion. The objections of such deficients, says Warfield, should no more be catered to in theology than would the objections of a color-blind person be catered to in the study of color in physics or the objections of a tone deaf person be catered to in the study of harmony in music. Warfield declares that "looseness of belief" is the "inevitable parent of looseness of practice." [28] The concern of these men is not that too much theology may quench the Christian's spirit but rather that too little will starve it.

By reversing the charge of legalism Machen turns the tables on those who subordinate doctrine. His argument runs along these lines. To insist upon the vital aspect of Christianity— that it is a new life—without complementing this with the forensic element—that justification is by faith—is to endanger or destroy the whole ethical character of Christianity, for it is the new standing before God through justification that gives moral significance to the new life.[29] By themselves the commands of God are a judgment on our failure and inability to obey them, and thus they necessitate the person of the Savior and the doctrine of salvation.[30] Ethical behavior is not faith in Christ but its effect, and faith itself is not a doing but a receiving.[31] The mark of child-like faith is conscious helplessness and a consequent willingness to receive a gift, and its simplicity is marred, not by knowledge but sometimes by ignorance and always by an admixture of self-trust.[32] However, if faith is thought of as essentially obedience to Christ, then salvation is not a gift of God but is obtained

[28] Warfield, *The Right of Systematic Theology*, pp. 27-28; *The Inspiration and Authority of the Bible*, p. 419.

[29] Machen, *What Is Faith?*, pp. 165-66.

[30] Machen, *The Christian View of Man*, pp. 11-13.

[31] Machen, *What Is Faith?*, pp. 88-89, 172-74. Cf. Kuyper, *The Work of the Holy Spirit*, pp. 320, 378, 420.

[32] Machen, *What Is Faith?*, pp. 94-96.

by obedience to the commands of Christ, and "such teaching is just a sublimated form of legalism." [33] This argument
introduces us to our next major topic, the concept of faith
as the means of appropriating revelation.

Before turning to the next section, let us note the symptoms
that we have encountered thus far of the malaise caused by
the non sequitur of propositional theology. We have seen
an attempt to be as undogmatic and as unlegalistic as possible,
and even a little bit of theological casuistry designed to tag
these undesirable labels on those who use them to describe
the position of propositional theology. And yet this is carried
on strictly within the confines of ameliorating a rigid form of
dogmatism and legalism. But if the propositional theologian
is unabashedly dogmatic and legalistic, on the grounds that
revealed propositions are to be believed and obeyed, why
should he wish to soften this characteristic and even charge
others with it? Is this just the avoidance of an extreme
position, or is it an expression of an unresolved conflict in
the position of propositional theology? Which of these two
possible explanations is applicable comes out most clearly in
an examination of the understanding in propositional theology
of the relation between faith as intellectual assent and faith
as trust.

The Appropriation of Revelation

The revelation recorded in the Bible and systematized in
theology is appropriated, or claimed for oneself, through the
exercise of faith. In examining the understanding of the
appropriation of revelation according to propositional theology,
we will consider its views of faith and knowledge, of faith as
assent and trust, and of the relation between faith and trust.

[33] Machen, *Christianity and Liberalism*, pp. 143-44.

FAITH AND KNOWLEDGE

Brunner contrasts the knowledge and truth of faith with other types of knowledge and truth. Propositional theologians do not recognize as sharp a difference as does Brunner and contend that faith is based upon knowledge and also issues in knowledge.[34]

Kuyper contends that since the term "faith" has been introduced mainly from the New Testament, and since secular literature seldom uses the term technically, it has been mistakenly restricted to religious discourse, especially in the area of soteriology, and has not been recognized as a pertinent concept in epistemology *(Erkenntnis-theorie)*.[35] Kuyper feels that the term "faith" should be employed in the formal sense, apart from all content. In this sense it would be seen clearly that faith, far from being antithetical to knowledge, is indispensable to knowledge, even to knowledge of visible things gained through sense perceptions and to knowledge gained discursively through logical demonstration, both of which depend on our willingness to believe the evidence. Of course, faith is abused when it caters to indolence by providing conviction concerning things which should be supported by the

[34] Machen, *What Is Faith?*, pp. 40, 229-35; Warfield, *Studies in Theology*, pp. 325-26. Warfield follows Augustine closely here. For a full treatment of Augustine's doctrine of faith and reason see B. B. Warfield, *Studies in Tertullian and Augustine* (New York: Oxford University Press, 1930), especially pp. 170-77, 389-92.

[35] Kuyper, *Principles of Sacred Theology*, p. 126. He points out that the biblical conception of faith does not exclude the more general (epistemological) usage, and indeed calls attention to it. He cites Heb. 11:1 as a key passage, and contends that "faith is here taken neither in an exclusively religious sense, much less in a soteriological significance, but very generally as an 'assurance' and 'proving' of objects which escape our perception, either because they do not yet exist (τὰ ἐλπιζόμενα), or because they do not show themselves (τὰ μὴ βλεπόμενα)" *(Ibid.,* pp. 126-27). On the other hand, Kuyper refers to Pythagorean literature and to Plutarch to illustrate that "the idea of taking up faith as a link in a demonstration was not entirely foreign to the ancients" *(Ibid)*.

162

more arduous tasks of observation and demonstration. But even though such abuse of faith should be reproved, the formal character of such faith is identical with that of faith properly understood. "Properly used or misused, faith is and always will be a means of becoming firmly convinced of a thing, and of making this conviction the starting-point of conduct, while for this conviction no empirical or demonstrative proof is offered or found." It should be noted that for Kuyper, even when we use the term "faith" to refer to the act of obtaining certainty immediately and directly as opposed to discursively, faith is contrasted with demonstration but not with knowing as such, since knowledge is not obtained exclusively by observation and demonstration.[36]

Warfield agrees with Kuyper that "faith" and "knowledge" are closely interrelated, but suggests that these terms may be employed to designate two different modes of conviction. The distinction for Warfield is that knowledge rests on reason and faith on authority. In knowledge the mode of conviction is our own perception or reason; in faith it is the testimony and authority of others. The difference is not in the nature of the ground of conviction, nor in the degree of certitude, but simply in the manner by which conviction is gained. "We cannot believe, any more than we can know, without adequate grounds; it is not faith but 'credulity' to accord credit to insufficient evidence; and an unreasonable faith is no faith at all." [37]

In short, Kuyper considers "faith" to be a formal term, designating a willingness to believe the evidence, and thus being relevant to all knowledge. Warfield places more emphasis on the content, and he believes that it is possible to distinguish between faith and knowledge on the basis that the designated conviction results proximately from different grounds, viz.

---

[36] *Ibid.*, pp. 125, 130-46, 384-89, 59-63, 128-29.
[37] Warfield, *Studies in Theology*, p. 326.

reason for knowledge and authority for faith. But both Kuyper, for whom the term "faith" is relevant to all knowledge, and Warfield, for whom the term "faith" is relevant to knowledge gained through authority but not through discursive reason, are agreed that faith is not opposed to knowledge but is a means of conviction and certitude concerning knowledge.

FAITH AS ASSENT

The understanding of faith as the source of conviction concerning knowledge is not incidental but basic to the propositional theologians' conception of faith. Correspondingly, faith is basically an attitude of assent, which may give rise to trust, whereas in encounter theology faith as assent and faith as trust are disparate.

In a philological appendix Warfield contends that the fundamental meanings of "faith"—fixedness, stability, steadfastness, reliability—are ultimately based on the concept of "holding" rather than "supporting," though he admits that the underlying concept must remain "somewhat doubtful." [38] In any case faith is an act of intellectual (not volitional) conviction. Faith is described as "a mental act or state to which we feel constrained by considerations objective to ourselves, or at least to the act or state in question," and as "a mental state or act which is determined by sufficient reasons." [39] To put it

[38] Warfield, *Biblical Foundations*, pp. 344 ff. Kuyper finds a similar etymological significance for the term "faith." Its root suggests "an action by which our consciousness is forced to surrender itself, and to hold something for true, to confide in something and to obey something" (*Principles of Sacred Theology*, p. 127). Our consciousness, at first unstable, uncertain, and tossed about, is checked by the exercise of the inescapable restraining power of faith, and consequently becomes stable, assured, and certain (*Ibid.*, pp. 127-28.)

[39] Warfield, *Studies in Theology*, pp. 313-14. Cf. pp. 318, 341-42.

succinctly, faith is not arbitrary but is an inescapable intellectual assent.

Although faith is always compelled by evidence, it does not follow that every faith or belief corresponds with reality, for our convictions can be fallible. To say that faith is a compelled consent "is not the same as saying that consent is produced only by compelling evidence, that is, evidence which is objectively adequate." Indeed, people vary in the amount, degree, and kind of evidence which is necessary to produce conviction, and even the same person will show variations in this regard. In other words, faith "does not follow the evidence itself . . ., but the judgment of the intellect on the evidence," which is highly subject to variation from one person to another, and from one state of the same intellect to another. Although faith is always compelled by evidence, it does not follow that the mind is a passive recipient of the evidence. Hence, adequacy of evidence to produce faith involves both objective and subjective adequacy. Faith is "not the mechanical result of the adduction of the evidence." And so, the concept of faith as consent forced by the evidence does not eliminate man's responsibility for his faith.[40]

One's faith or creed is effective only as long as it is believed to be true, and if the subsequent increase of knowledge should indicate that the object of our trust is unworthy of it, our faith in the person is destroyed.[41] It is on the necessity of true knowledge about God and Jesus Christ that Christian scholarship rests.[42] A false faith may produce many benefits, Machen admits, but these benefits do not make the faith true. "Though it has transformed the world from darkness to light,

[40] Warfield, *Studies in Theology*, pp. 318-19, 335-57. Cf. Packer, *"Fundamentalism" and the Word of God*, pp. 123-25.

[41] Machen, *What Is Faith?*, pp. 93, 175-77; *Christianity and Liberalism*, pp. 141-43.

[42] Machen, *What Is Christianity?*, p. 123.

though it has produced thousands of gloriously healthy lives, it remains a pathological phenomenon. It is false, and sooner or later it is sure to be found out."[43] As a counterfeit, false faith should be detected and removed from circulation; yet false faith does not deny but rather presumes genuine faith. We must distinguish between the utility of faith and the truth of faith.

Faith as Trust

The concept of faith as trust is not at all eliminated by the emphasis of propositional theology on faith as assent, for this tradition sees no opposition or tension between these two aspects of faith. The element of trust is thought of as being present in every act of knowing, though it is more prominent in religious knowledge.[44] Trust, by its very nature, involves dependence on a person. Such dependence, which is basic to religion, gives acts of faith their religious quality "and raises them from mere beliefs of propositions, the contents of which happen to be of religious purport, to acts possessed of religious character."[45] Trust involves an attitude of reverence and love based on firm and unshaken conviction in the trustworthiness of another person, and produces an utter commitment.[46]

The propositional theologian cannot fairly be charged with having so emphasized assent that he has eliminated the element of trust in his conception of faith. Consider, for example,

[43] Machen, *Christianity and Liberalism,* p. 143.

[44] Warfield, *Studies in Theology,* p. 329. "Matters of faith, matters of belief are different from matters of knowledge—not as convictions less clear, firm, or well-grounded, not as convictions resting on grounds less objectively valid, not as convictions determined rather by desire, will, than by evidence—but as convictions resting on grounds less direct and immediate to the soul, and therefore involving a more prominent element of trust, in a word, as convictions grounded in authority, testimony as distinguished from convictions grounded in rational proof" (*Ibid.,* p. 330). Cf. Packer, *"Fundamentalism" and the Word of God,* pp. 115-16.

[45] *Ibid.,* p. 331.

[46] Warfield, *Biblical Foundations,* p. 316.

Kuyper's assertion that faith "is the daring breaking of our
unity into a duality; placing of another ego over against our
own ego; and the courage to face that distinction because
our ego finds its point of support and of rest only in that
other ego." Warfield also emphasizes the element of trust.
"Religious faith does not reach its height in assent to propositions of whatever religious content and however well fitted to
call out religious trust, but comes to its rights only when
it rests with adoring trust on a person." The dependence on
and commitment to God or Jesus Christ may become all-
encompassing. Indeed, it may "absorb the prior implication of
crediting almost altogether." This significant assertion of Warfield deserves development in his own words.

Faith in God, and above all, faith in Jesus Christ, is just trust
in him in its purity. Thus in its higher applications the element
of trust which is present in faith in all its applications . . . finishes
by becoming well-nigh the entire connotation of the term; and "to
believe in," "to have faith in" comes to mean simply "entrust your-
self to." When "faith" can come thus to mean just "trust" we cannot wonder that it is the implication of "trust" in the term which
rules its usage and determines its applications throughout the
whole course of its development.[47]

RELATION BETWEEN ASSENT AND TRUST

For propositional theologians, faith is trust based on assent.
Although they agree with encounter theologians that faith
involves personal relation, they would not agree that God
cannot be personally trusted on the basis of ideas or knowledge.

Warfield accepts the traditional Protestant analysis of faith
as involving *notitia, assensus,* and *fiducia.* While he grants

[47] Kuyper, *Principles of Sacred Theology,* p. 266; Warfield, *Studies in
Theology,* pp. 331-32.

that the stress of this definition is on the fiducial element, he considers this due to the fact that it contrasts with the Roman Catholic limitation of faith to intellectual assent, and he adds that traditionally, though not universally, Protestants have not eliminated the elements of understanding and assent.[48]

Trust depends on and develops from assent. Although faith is thought of as being fulfilled in personal relation between man and God, it is considered a mistake to think that this is the beginning of faith rather than its mature form. Faith, as a means of obtaining certainty, is the foundation on which trust or confidence is built. Religious faith is formed by the production of trust through assent. If we feel certain that another person is a man of integrity, we trust him as an immediate result; if we are not certain, we do not trust him.[49]

With those who regard faith as saving trust in Christ, Warfield expresses "the fullest agreement that saving faith is a matter not of the intellect but of the heart, that it is 'confidence' rather than 'conviction.'" However, he does not agree with the presentation of this in the form of the strict alternative between trust and intellectual assent, as is characteristic of encounter theology. For Warfield, trust rests upon a conviction, gained through evidence, of the trustworthiness of the object of trust. So it is not necessary, Warfield contends, to remove the propositional element from faith in order to avoid the view that mere intellectual assent is adequate apart from personal submission. Assent is possible without full development into trust, but there can be no trust without prior knowledge and assent.[50]

[48] Warfield, *Studies in Theology*, pp. 340-41.
[49] Kuyper, *Principles of Sacred Theology*, p. 391; *The Work of the Holy Spirit*, pp. 384-401; B. B. Warfield, *Christology and Criticism* (New York: Oxford University Press, 1929), pp. 361-67; *Studies in Theology*, pp. 340-42. Cf. Packer, *"Fundamentalism" and the Word of God*, pp. 116-19.
[50] Warfield, *Studies in Theology*, pp. 334-37.

Machen contends that, simple though it may seem, communion between persons is a complex phenomenon, often resting upon years of observation. Likewise, communion with God and with Jesus Christ may seem simple and untheological, but it is a complex phenomenon, resting upon God's self-revelation and his provision of salvation.[51]

The proverbial "simple faith" of the child is based upon experiences with the person who is trusted, and no child will trust a person whom he considers untrustworthy. Machen describes the faith of those who insist on trust apart from assent as "a very subtle, sophisticated, unchildlike thing" and adds: "What is really childlike is the faith that is founded upon knowledge of the one in whom trust is reposed." The infant's intellect may be inoperative before conscious personal life has arisen, but Machen does not believe that this is the stage to which Christian faith ought to return in obedience to the Lord's command to receive the kingdom as little children.[52] How, then, do we receive the kingdom?

Knowledge, Machen insists, is a necessary prerequisite to trust in Jesus Christ. To state it negatively, we cannot trust a person about whom we assent to propositions that make him untrustworthy.[53] For example, one would not entrust his money to a known swindler on the basis that faith in a person is independent of knowledge about him. Likewise, there can be no trust in God if one believes him either nonexistent or untrustworthy. Let us interrupt the exposition of Machen's thoughts here to note that one can, nonetheless, trust a God whom one holds with the mind to be incapable of adequate

---

[51] Machen, *What Is Faith?*, pp. 36-37, 92-93; *Christianity and Liberalism*, pp. 54-55. "Human affection, apparently so simple, is really just bristling with dogma. It depends upon a host of observations treasured up in the mind with regard to the character of our friends" (*Christianity and Liberalism*, p. 55-56). Cf. *The Christian Faith in the Modern World*, p. 118.

[52] Machen, *What Is Faith?*, pp. 94-95. Cf. Kuyper, *Principles of Sacred Theology*, p. 130, and Buber on the "inborn Thou."

[53] *Ibid.*, pp. 48, 89-90, 97; *What Is Christianity?*, p. 120.

expression in propositional statements. Returning to Machen, and stating his thesis now positively, we have faith in a person only on the basis of some knowledge about him which makes our confidence seem reasonable.[54] The significance of this position is brought out clearly and forcefully in Machen's comment on Heb. 11:6: "He that cometh to God must believe that he is, and *that* he is a rewarder of them that diligently seek him." (KJV)

Religion is here made to depend absolutely upon doctrine; the one who comes to God must not only believe *in* a person, but he must also believe *that* something is true; faith is here declared to involve acceptance of a proposition. There could be no plainer insistence upon the doctrinal or intellectual basis of faith. It is impossible, according to the Epistle to the Hebrews, to have faith in a person without accepting with the mind the facts about the person.[55]

Again, since we must know that Jesus Christ has saved us in order to trust him as Savior, doctrine is not merely a reflection upon, but the basis of, our personal relationships to him.[56]

Trust may be more than acceptance of a creed or proposition, but it necessarily involves this. "Faith is essentially dogmatic. Despite all you can do, you cannot remove the element of intellectual assent from it." [57] When people speak

[54] *Ibid.*, pp. 46-47, 52, 75, 77-78, 88; *What Is Christianity?*, p. 120-21; *Christianity and Liberalism*, pp. 54-55.

[55] Machen, *What Is Faith?*, p. 47. Cf. pp. 149-51.

[56] *Ibid.*, pp. 143-44, 151-54, 161; *What Is Christianity?*, pp. 122-23, 277-78; *The Christian View of Man*, pp. 13-14; Warfield, *Christology and Criticism*, p. 259.

[57] Machen, *Christianity and Liberalism*, p. 142. Cf. "though revelation involves a personal encounter with God, yet the rational faculty is always supremely active in the encounter" (Jewett, "Special Revelation as Historical and Personal," in Henry, *Revelation and the Bible*, p. 55). Cf. also Packer, *"Fundamentalism" and the Word of God*, pp. 42-43.

of trust in Jesus being possible apart from the theological interpretation of his death and resurrection, they do not really mean trust but admiration or reverence. Admiration, reverence, even mother love are subhuman or nonpersonal and amoral if they are independent of some knowledge.[58] It is the exercise of trust in the light of the knowledge one has about the other person that raises it to the personal level, and trust is possible only between persons.

Since Machen has defended knowledge as necessary to trust, he must deal with the question of how much knowledge is necessary. He asserts that a very small amount of knowledge is often, indeed normally, sufficient for faith. What Machen is insisting upon is that knowledge logically precedes faith, even though it may be possible for them to coincide chronologically in some cases. Nonetheless, the more knowledge the better. As a matter of fact, Machen contends that we today are in need of more knowledge about Jesus in order to trust him than was necessary for those to whom he was bodily present.[59]

Consequently, for propositional theology, the Bible is indispensable as a collection of accurate facts about Jesus Christ. In speaking of our debt to the Bible, Warfield says:

We may say that without a Bible we might have had Christ and all that he stands for to our souls. Let us not say that this might not have been possible. But neither let us forget that, in point of fact, it is to the Bible that we owe it that we know Christ and are found in him. And may it not be fairly doubted whether you and I,—however it may have been with others,—would have had Christ had there been no Bible?[60]

[58] *Ibid.*, pp. 44, 54-55; *The Christian Faith in the Modern World,* pp. 118-20.
[59] Machen, *What Is Faith?*, pp. 91-94, 161; *What Is Christianity?*, pp. 120-23.
[60] Warfield, *The Inspiration and Authority of the Bible,* p. 126.

Indeed, it is Warfield's contention that the Bible contains "the only authentic records" of the revelation of God through Jesus Christ.[61] Machen chides those who say that they have the present Christ, and so care nothing about the dead documents of the past. "Without the Bible you would never have known so much as whether there be any Christ. Yet now that you have Christ you give the Bible up." [62] The factual content of the Bible is essential to our knowledge of Jesus Christ.

However, we need not only an historical account of facts concerning the life of Jesus Christ but also an immediate, personal relation.[63] Machen believes that the Bible meets this need also. In the gospel record "we see not merely a lifeless picture, but receive the impression of a living Person," and we can share in the experiences that his contemporaries had in his physical presence.[64] The Bible not only tells us what manner of person Jesus Christ was but also makes it possible for us to come in contact with him today.[65] So important is this aspect of personal relation for Kuyper that he considers it incorrect to say that we come to the Scripture first, and through it to Christ. What he means by this is that mere reading of the Bible is not sufficient, and only after a person has been regenerated by Christ does the Scripture become meaningful to him as a source of revelation.[66] Even so, after regeneration the believer finds it impossible to resist the Scripture.[67] We both come to Christ by means of the Scripture and come to the Scripture by means of Christ.

[61] Warfield, *Studies in Theology*, p. 60.

[62] Machen, *What Is Christianity?*, p. 183. Cf. pp. 103-4.

[63] Machen, *Christianity and Liberalism*, p. 43.

[64] *Ibid.*, p. 40.

[65] Machen, *What Is Christianity?*, pp. 31-33.

[66] Kuyper, *Principles of Sacred Theology*, pp. 551-53, 557-59; *Calvinism*, pp. 57-58.

[67] "If, then, finally, the believer goes back to the first stage in his Christian life, i.e., to his personal faith in his Saviour, and realizes that Christ himself has presented the Holy Scripture—which the common opinion in the com-

THE NON SEQUITUR OF PROPOSITIONAL THEOLOGY

The Value and Distortion of Propositional Theology

The view of propositional theology concerning appropriated revelation (faith), which we have just examined, has some valuable insights, but it is vitiated by a non sequitur. If we are to preserve its values we must expose the non sequitur that leads from a recognition of propositional elements in revelation to a theory of propositional revelation. Neither the theory of propositional revelation nor the theory of revelation as encounter, which denies propositional elements, has offered a satisfactory account of how revelation yields doctrine. An adequate solution to this problem depends upon an analysis which enables us to follow the tradition of propositional theology in the recognition of propositional elements in revelation but not in its description of revelation as propositional.

The key issue at this point is that of the relation between trust and assent. For encounter theology, trust is in the dimension of I-Thou relations and assent is in the dimension of I-It connections. For propositional theology, trust and assent are combined, but faith is understood as primarily an act of intellect rather than of will. However, as we have noted, it is clearly recognized that religious faith finds its highest expression in personal trust. Assent and trust are rendered compatible by conceiving of trust as depending on and developing from assent. The basic argument is that we trust another person on the basis of our knowledge that he is a man of

munion of saints has adopted in its world of thought as theopneustic, and of the Divine *truth* of which, thanks to the 'Witness of the Holy Spirit,' he is himself firmly convinced—as the product of the Holy Spirit, the assurance of his faith on this point is immovably established (Kuyper, *Principles of Sacred Theology,* p. 562). The Bible is thus essential as the means by which the essence of Christ is brought to us *(Ibid.,* p. 477). "Faith and Scripture belong together; the Holy Spirit intended the one for the other" (Kuyper, *The Work of the Holy Spirit,* p. 419). Faith in a Christ of the imagination would lead to error, and so, in Calvin's terms, "Christ in the garments of the Sacred Scripture" is the only object of faith *(Ibid.,* pp. 397, 420).

integrity. The conclusion drawn by propositional theology is that faith is basically intellectual assent to a proposition and and trust is absolutely dependent upon doctrine. Thus we may describe the situation in propositional theology as a recognition of the meaning and significance of faith as trust in a person but a failure to develop the concept of revelation in the light of this recognition.[68]

How can we account for this failure? Let us retrace our steps. The propositional theologian argues that we cannot trust a person whom we do not know to be a man of integrity, and consequently, knowledge is a necessary prerequisite to faith in Jesus Christ. Here we can agree. Dietrich Bonhoeffer was keenly sensitive to this issue, for he lived and died in circumstances in which one entrusted his very life to others. In such circumstances he says: "We have learnt never to trust a scoundrel an inch, but to give ourselves to the trustworthy without reserve." [69] We do not entrust our money to men whom we know to have been swindlers unless we have very strong evidence (overruling knowledge) of a change of attitude. Our trust in, and commitment to, Jesus Christ is not a result of blind faith but is based on a conviction of his trustworthiness, which is gained by knowledge about him. In this sense, knowledge is logically prior to faith. But, because of their belief in an infallible Bible as a source book of theology, the propositional theologians draw the conclusion that faith is dependent upon belief in correct doctrine. We may agree with them that there can be no trust in Jesus Christ without some prior knowledge about him that warrants our trust. But we disagree that this knowledge must necessarily be in doctrinal form and contend rather that it is an existential,

[68] Cf. Rudolf Bultmann, *Existence and Faith,* tr. by Schubert M. Ogden (New York: Meridian, 1960), pp. 66-67. Cf. also the discussion of "Faith as Venture," *Ibid.,* pp. 55-57.

[69] *Letters and Papers from Prison,* p. 28.

personal kind of knowledge that is prerequisite. Consideration of the nature of this existential, personal kind of knowledge will be the concern of the final chapter in which I present an emended view of the analogy of encounter. But at this point we may express agreement with the essence of the argument of propositional theology that trust involves assent, but disagreement with the kind of assent insisted upon by this tradition.

7. How Revelation as Encounter Yields Doctrine

We have argued that neither encounter theology nor propositional theology provides an adequate account of how revelation yields doctrine. When encounter theology was seen to be inadequate, we turned to the position of propositional theology. We further explored the possibility of emending this latter position and found that this was not possible. But we have not yet determined whether or not the position of encounter theology is emendable.

The task of this final chapter is to resolve the current impasse in the understanding of how revelation yields doctrine. To say with the unemended form of encounter theology that I-It knowledge is always subsequent to revelation as encounter is to establish a divergence between revelation and doctrine that cannot be bridged in theory nor observed in practice. On the other hand, to say with propositional theology that revelation is the disclosure of propositions is to so identify revelation and doctrine as to lose viability in theory and charity in practice. In its strength propositional theology has shown us that propositional elements cannot be ignored, but in its weakness it has shown us that they cannot infallibly imparted. In its strength encounter theology has shown us the primacy of personal trust over intellectual assent, but in its weakness it, too, has shown us that propositional elements cannot be ignored. This indicates that the way ahead involves an incorporation of I-It elements within the basic I-Thou encounter with God. The value of such an emended form of encounter theology is that it allows for the incorporation of I-It knowledge within encounter, and for the use of scientific and ontological knowledge as sources in the task of theological construction. The view that is developed here is in contrast with the relegation of I-It knowledge to a separate and subordinate sphere, as in the unemended form of encounter theology, and also in contrast with the elevation of assent so that it absorbs trust, as in propositional theology.

Brunner's distinction between I-Thou and I-It has ramifications that extend beyond his theory of revelation. Let us consider, as examples, the import of the radical disjunction between I-Thou and I-It for Brunner's ecclesiology and ethics. In Brunner's ecclesiology *(The Misunderstanding of the Church* and the section "Ekklesia and Church" in *The Christian Doctrine of the Church, Faith, and the Consummation)* we find a sharp contrast between the Christian Ekklesia as a dynamic fellowship of the people of God and the development of the institutional life of the church. The church as an institution, though a necessary "instrument and shell" of the Ekklesia, is not simply an inadequate means of expressing the Christian fellowship but is actually a misunderstanding of the nature of the Christian fellowship. However, if I-It elements are incorporated within the I-Thou encounter with God, then it is possible to see the institutional and other structures of the church as constructive expressions of Christian community, although they may militate against as well as promote genuine Christian fellowship. A second example of this dualism is found in Brunner's ethics (especially his earliest work in this field *The Divine Imperative*). He describes the difference between the natural orders and the commandment of love as "an insoluble dualism,"[1] again theoretically denying the possibility of constructive interrelation between the impersonal (natural orders) and the personal (commandment of love).

Defending anonymity as essential for preserving the possibility of human relationships, Harvey Cox suggests the use of "I-you" as an intermediate term to be added to the dichotomy, "I-Thou" and "I-It."[2] Cox notes that Buber never claimed that all our relationships could be in the I-Thou mode, yet he feels that the failure to provide an intermediate term has led to the misuse of his categories by others. The "I-you" relation, Cox urges, is especially important for understanding the city, for in this milieu there are many public relationships that have a personal, rather than I-It, quality, even though they are not allowed to develop into the intensity of I-Thou. The danger Cox mentions is that without the I-you category any relationship that is not intense will be relegated to I-It. But there is also the danger that an insistence upon the personal nature of more superficial relations will result in a devaluation of I-Thou, so that it is used to refer to a friendly attitude to a clerk or a smile for a delivery boy rather than being reserved for more intimate relationships. However, I would reject Cox's later suggestion that the "I-you" relation be employed as an additional analogy for our relation to God.[3] This would mean that we can have a more intimate and intense relationship with other human

---

[1] Emil Brunner, *The Divine Imperative* (Philadelphia: Westminister, 1947), p. 222.

[2] *The Secular City* (New York: Macmillan, 1965), pp. 39-49.

[3] *Ibid.*, pp. 263-65.

beings than we do with God. The confrontation of God is not adequately expressed by the authentically personal, but restricted, sense of mutuality that comes from working together on a team, or other such I-you situations.

The fact that Buber did his thinking in the German language has exerted a decisive limitation on the formulation of I-Thou philosophy. In the German language the use of the word "Thou" is an expression of intimacy, reserved for relatives and close friends, which makes it an appropriate bearer of Buber's meaning. However, the German language makes no clear distinction between person and thing in the third person. For Buber, it makes little or no difference whether we say "I-he," "I-she" or "I-it." [4] Because of his use of the German language, Buber could speak clearly and appropriately about persons only in the second person. The English language, however, can use the phrase "I-he" to refer to a personal relationship to one who is absent. In other words, it refers to an I-Thou relationship as it is remembered. So, an I-Thou relationship does not have to fade into the distorted (because impersonal) I-It but can become an I-he relationship. Consequently, the affirmation "He is the Christ" can be fully as personal as the affirmation "Thou art the Christ." At the very least we need to insist upon the notion of "I-he" and "I-she" relations as a supplement to "I-Thou." But the ambition of this chapter is to go even beyond this to assert that I-It (impersonal) elements are essentially involved in man's encounter with God.

By contending that encounter with God includes I-It elements, we are not altering the notion of encounter but the method of applying it to our knowledge of God. In other words, we are saying that encounter with God is like encounter

[4] Buber, *I and Thou,* p. 3. For the insights into the possibilities of the I-he concept, I am indebted to Dr. Gordon D. Kaufman, although I must take full responsibility for the elaboration and expression of it.

179

with man in that both incorporate I-It elements within a basic I-Thou relation. However, since the absence of I-It elements in divine-human encounter was the basis of the modification of the analogy in its use by Buber and Brunner, it is incumbent upon us, at the outset, to determine a new principle of modification. We have not emended but destroyed the analogy unless we establish a new principle of modification to replace the discarded notion of the purity of divine-human encounter that Buber and Brunner have employed.

Paul van Buren contends that the theological use of analogical language is meaningless. His basic argument is that in Rudolf Bultmann and Schubert Ogden, all talk about God is really talk about man. For example, van Buren claims that the assertion "God loves me" is equivalent to "I feel secure." [5] Encounter theologians might well be inclined to agree that the subjectivism of the tradition criticized by van Buren is such that statements about God can be translated without remainder into statements about man. But they cannot evade van Buren's challenge, for he is not simply attacking subjectivism in theology but is rejecting the use of analogical language in theology as meaningless. But this challenge may place van Buren on even shakier ground than he wants to occupy. For, unless van Buren really is advocating nothing more than a humanist view of life, the very phrase, "the secular meaning of the Gospel," is analogical and needs to be analyzed as such. We may need to reject some analogies, but our first effort should be to reform them.

If encounter theology is adjudged emendable by means of the use of a new principle of modification for the analogy, we can then proceed to a new understanding of how revelation yields doctrine. In the development of this consideration,

[5] Paul M. van Buren, *The Secular Meaning of the Gospel* (New York: Macmillan, 1963), pp. 65-68. See chap. 4 for his discussion of various linguistic analyses of theological language.

attention is given to semantical theories which emphasize the nature of language as an expression of both knowledge and feeling. The nature of an existential, personal knowledge, proposed to be present in encounter, is then elaborated as an objective element in revelation. This view of revelation is contrasted with the emphasis of propositional theology on doctrinal assent, which absorbs the element of trust, and with the emphasis of unemended encounter theology on trust, which relegates objective knowledge to a separate and subordinate sphere.

A New Principle of Modification for the Analogy

If we are to retain encounter as an analogy of our relation with God, we must demonstrate a successful way of modifying the concept of encounter between humans so that it will point toward divine-human encounter. Any workable principle of modification would enable us to proceed, but the one I would like to propose is that encounter with God is distinguished from encounter with persons on the basis of the contrast between the infinitude of God and finitude of man.

Where and how are we to apply this principle of modification? Encounter between humans involves two dimensions, viz. somatic (the body) and psychic (the self-transcending, free self). Perception of the somatic dimension may not establish encounter, for it may not go beyond categories of height and weight, symptoms, case study, and so forth. But when we see through these manifestations into the mystery of personality and become aware that we are in relation with a self-transcending, free self in all the particularity of his unique personality, then we have established relation. Our principle of modification is applicable to both the somatic and psychic dimensions. Let us explore this application in order to see how encounter with the infinite might be differentiated from encounter with finite persons, even if both include I-It elements.

The somatic dimension of encounter is modified in our relation with God in both the form of God's embodiment and in the means by which the "self" of God is expressed through embodiment. If we say that God is embodied and reveals himself through this medium, we are speaking analogically.

The embodiment of God is not the same as possession of a body. When we say that God is embodied we do not mean he has a body with a head, arms, and legs. For men embodiment means localization, but God is not confined to a particular spot or area. He is not here, rather than there. Human attachment to a body means that man is faced with limitations all through life, and ultimately with the final thwarting of realization of purpose through death. God is not contingent being but is rather that self-sufficient being on whom we depend. Yet there is a basis of similarity. We speak of God's embodiment because, as we do with persons, we glimpse God's selfhood through external manifestations. Just as we attempt to know other persons through interpretation of their behavior, so we approach knowledge of God through interpretation of his "mighty acts." [6]

Just what, specifically, is the "body" of God through which we observe him? We must beware of a tempting oversimplification at this point. It is easy to consider the means by which we come to knowledge of God—especially Jesus Christ, the church as the continuing body of Christ, and the Bible—to be the "body" of God, through which he manifests himself. But this oversimplification would not be adequate because it would involve spatial limitations, no matter how much the area

---

[6] For a discussion of the difficulties involved in interpretation of the "mighty acts of God," see Langdon B. Gilkey, "Cosmology, Ontology, and the Travail of Biblical Language," *The Journal of Religion,* July, 1961, pp. 194-205.

and mobility were increased over that of man. God would be less spatially restricted than man, but still restricted. Such a conception of the embodiment of God is incomplete. We must say further that the God whom we come to know through such special manifestations is the God who is the source of all being. When we come to know God through his embodiment in special revelatory acts, we realize that the embodiment through which we came to know him does not exhaust his embodiment. We become aware that the God whom we know through Jesus Christ is the God who reveals himself in every event, though we can see him in every event only after we have seen him in the special events through which he manifested himself. The work of Pierre Teilhard de Chardin, who incorporates science within a religious style of life, is very instructive at the point of understanding the earth as the "bodily" expression of God.

There is also a difference in the way in which God and man reveal themselves through embodiment. Human embodiment implies the possibility of unconscious, or even unwilling, self-disclosure. For example, men may reveal themselves willy-nilly through such manifestations as facial expression (e. g., lifting the eyebrows or smiling), body movements (e. g., shrugging the shoulders or slamming a door), complexion (e. g., blushing or turning pale), and voice quality (e. g., quavering and breathless or snarling). But God's self-disclosure is always a conscious activity. We cannot discern his anger by a snarling voice, nor his pleasure by a smile. We cannot even formulate a plan of action and ask God to express his approval by tapping two times or his disapproval by tapping three times. Nor, as Job insisted, can we infer God's pleasure from prosperity or his displeasure from adversity. The rain is no sign of his purpose, will, or intention, for it falls indiscriminately on the just and the unjust. We cannot infer God's nature on the basis of his general activity but must depend on his self-manifestation through unique events. This means, in traditional language, that natural revelation does not give us adequate knowledge of God, and that we are dependent on special revelation. In short, knowledge of God must be received as a gift.

The mediation of encounter in the psychic dimension is also modified. For our understanding of other human persons we rely heavily on our own self-understanding.[7] This accounts for the greater difficulty in communication with, and greater possibility for misunderstanding of, those who are of a different nationality or culture. In such a case many of the clues that are so helpful in understanding persons whose situation is very similar with our own become either valueless or, even worse, of negative value, so that we do not merely fail to understand but misunderstand. Augustine goes so far as to say that it is easier to communicate with one's own dog than with foreigners. Difficulty of communication and misunderstanding are possible between persons of similar background, but the possibility increases in direct ratio with the increase of dissimilarity. In the case of encounter with God, the distance is so vast that the difficulty of communication and the possibility of misunderstanding reach their zenith. Therefore the elements which are common to man and God cannot be transferred to one another without modification.

An appeal to the image of God in man does not seem to be very helpful as a practical guide for this modification since there is great diversity of opinion as to what constitutes the image of God in man, and also as to the effect that the fall of man has had on the image of God within him.[8] But we encounter another person as a self-transcending, free self. Let

[7] Cf. Karl Heim, *Christian Faith and Natural Science,* tr. by N. Horton Smith (New York: Harper & Row, 1953), pp. 71-81.

[8] For a survey of historical and contemporary views see David Cairns, *The Image of God in Man* (New York: Philosophical Library, 1953).

us seek to differentiate between finite and infinite "transcendence" and "freedom."

Self-transcendence in man means that he is not simply determined by the structures of the self and its position in nature and history. But even when man frees himself from determinism by such structures, he remains dependent and finite within the structures of space and time. However, God's infinite transcendence frees him not only from determinism by such structures but from the structures themselves. As Tillich puts it, God "is the creative ground of the spatial structure of the world, but he is not bound to the structure, positively or negatively." [9]

In the context of God's transcendence, Tillich says that the holy God is "quite other," but adds that God's otherness "is not really conceived as otherness if it remains in the aesthetic-cognitive realm and is not experienced as the otherness of the divine 'Thou' whose freedom may conflict with my freedom." [10] The freedom of one man and another may conflict, and yet they share freedom as part of a common humanity. Likewise, the freedom of God and man may conflict, but it is nonetheless common to both God and man. But the term "freedom," like the term "transcendence," has a different meaning when applied to man and God and cannot therefore serve as a basis of simple comparison of man and God without modification. In affirming the freedom of God we affirm that he is self-sufficient and unconditioned. [11] Man's freedom, by way of contrast, is understood within a context of man as a contingent being whose actions are determined from one perspective, though man is free to decide and act in accord

[9] Tillich, *Systematic Theology*, I, 263.
[10] *Ibid.*
[11] *Ibid.*, p. 248.

with a chosen purpose.[12] The freedom of finite man and the freedom of the infinite God are sufficiently different that although we can speak of them as common elements shared by both, we cannot apply the term univocally to God and man. We can, however, apply the term analogically to God and man.

The distinction between finite and infinite may be successfully substituted for the inadequate distinction between pure and impure "Thous" as a principle of modification of encounter so that it serves as an analogy of the relation between man and God. We are able to grant that encounters with God involve I-It elements and still distinguish between encounters with persons and with God. Encounter theology, unlike propositional theology, is able to be emended.

A New Understanding of How Revelation Yields Doctrine

If, as we have contended, encounter theology is able to be emended so as to include I-It elements in encounter with God, then we can explore the solution of the problem of how revelation yields doctrine. As a first step in this direction let us discuss the nature of language as an expression of both feeling and knowledge.

Before we begin this analysis it should be noted that those whose theories we will be discussing (R. G. Collingwood and Susanne K. Langer) develop them in opposition to the logical positivist dichotomy between the "scientific" and "emotive" use of language.[13] Despite radical differences there is a strange congruence between logical positivism and propositional theology in their insistence that language must be used to express

---

[12] For a discussion of man's freedom as the power to bind time and its interdependence with determinism, see Gordon D. Kaufman, *The Context of Decision* (Nashville: Abingdon Press, 1961), pp. 76-80.

[13] A classic statement of this distinction is found in C. K. Ogden and I. A. Richards, *The Meaning of Meaning* (New York: Harcourt, Brace & Co., 1923). See especially the chapter "Symbol Situations."

only that which is clear and factual, or else it is meaningless.[14] Both firmly insist that there is either objective truth or no truth at all. But the semantical theories we will consider also challenge the encounter theologians, who separate the language of trust and assent into different spheres. If language can include expression of both objective meaning and feeling, as we shall see Collingwood and Langer argue, it would seem that neither propositional theology nor unemended encounter theology are adequate expressions of the nature of language.

Collingwood has attacked the traditional view that language is primarily informative (scientific) and derivatively expressive. He contends that language is a "feature of experience at the conscious level," and that it is originally imaginative and expressive and never loses these characteristics, although it does become modified to serve the purposes of intellect.[15] He insists that language is not a tool that we can use either to make assertions (true or false, i.e., to express propositions) or to express emotion. This is an erroneous dichotomy. We are not forced either to search for objective truth or to abandon that search altogether and speak rather of subjective emotions. Collingwood criticizes Richards' classic distinction between the "scientific" and "emotive" use of language. Collingwood does agree with Richards that thought and emotion are two forces which produce tension, but he further insists that it is not a disruptive tension. Collingwood maintains that scientific discourse is a specialized and derivative form of language which is especially adapted to serve the purposes of the intellect.

Two lines of attack are employed against the complete separation of scientific and emotive use of language. Collingwood's

[14] See Gordon H. Clark, "Special Divine Revelation as Rational," and William J. Martin, "Special Revelation as Objective," in Henry, *Revelation and the Bible*, pp. 39-41, 61-72.

[15] R. G. Collingwood, *The Principles of Art* (New York: Oxford University Press, 1938), pp. 225-41.

first argument[16] against such a dichotomy is that even when a person is making a determined effort to state a truth, it is impossible to avoid an element of emotional expressiveness, indicated by such means as choice of words and tone of voice. He expressed his conclusion thus: " 'The proposition,' understood as a form of words expressing thought and not emotion, and as constituting the unit of scientific discourse, is a fictitious entity." Collingwood's second argument is that thought or intellect has its appropriate emotions, which must receive expression in intellectualized language.[17] Thus he rejects the sharp division between language which expresses scientific fact and language which expresses subjective experience. Even though symbols can be developed for strictly scientific purposes, with no expression of emotion, Collingwood insists that once symbolism is mastered and used, "it reacquires the emotional expressiveness of language proper." Collingwood speaks of symbolism as "intellectualized language: language, because it expresses emotions; intellectualized, because adapted to the expression of intellectual emotions."

A position similar to Collingwood's has been supported by Langer. She, too, refuses to make a sharp dichotomy between feeling and knowledge. She insists, rather, that feeling participates in knowledge and understanding.[18]

She has given special attention to the "symbolic transformation of experiences." Langer considers the active translation of experiences into symbols as a "basic process in the human

[16] *Ibid.*, pp. 264-66.

[17] *Ibid.*, pp. 266-69. His principle is summed up in these words: "If it is once granted that intellectualized language does express emotion, and that this emotion is not a vague or generalized emotion, but the perfectly definite emotion proper to a perfectly definite act of thought, the consequence follows that in expressing the emotion the act of thought is expressed too. There is no need for two separate expressions, one of the thought and the other of the emotion accompanying it. There is only one expression" *(Ibid.*, p. 267).

[18] Susanne K. Langer, *Philosophy in a New Key* (Cambridge: Harvard University Press, 1951), pp. 96-102.

brain," as a "law of the brain," which "carries on a constant process of ideation," and as a "fulfillment of a basic need." [19] The experiences gained through the senses are symbolized, and the resulting symbols are the person's elementary ideas.

Some of these ideas can be combined and manipulated in the manner we call "reasoning." Others do not lend themselves to this use, but are naturally telescoped into dreams, or vapor off in conscious fantasy; and a vast number of them build the most typical and fundamental edifice of the human mind—religion.[20]

Symbolic transformation takes place in two modes. The two symbolic modes are verbal (discursive) and nonverbal. The primary virtue of language (the verbal mode) is denotation, but there is a symbolism which is purely connotative, a prime example of which is music.[21] It is interesting in this regard to note Evelyn Underhill's remark that if the mystic were a musician he could communicate his experience much more clearly in terms of that art than through verbal language.[22] Langer insists that the significance of music is semantic not symptomatic. She supports this contention by arguing that the meaning of music is not

that of a stimulus to evoke emotions, nor that of a signal to announce them; if it has an emotional content, it "has" it in the same sense that language "has" its conceptual content—*symbolically*. It is not usually derived *from* affects nor intended *for* them; but we must say, with certain reservations, that it is *about* them.

---

[19] *Ibid.*, pp. 41-44. Cf. the definition of man as an *"animal symbolicum,"* rather than an *"animal rationale"* (Ernst Cassirer, *An Essay on Man* [New Haven: Yale University Press, 1944], p. 26).

[20] *Ibid.*, p. 42.

[21] *Ibid.*, p. 101.

[22] *Mysticism* (New York: Meridian, 1955), p. 76. Cf. p. 336. Underhill explains that verbal language corresponds to the physical world and is thus not convenient for speaking of the transcendental world, for a description of which see *Ibid.*, pp. 55-56.

Music is not the cause or the cure of feelings, but their *logical expression;* though even in this capacity it has special ways of functioning, that make it incommensurable with language, and even with presentational symbols like images, gestures, and rites.[23]

To sum up, the semantical theory described here holds that experience undergoes symbolic transformation and that the resultant symbols express both feeling and objective meaning.

These theories of Collingwood and Langer, which argue forcefully that feeling and thought are inseparable in our conscious response to life, suggest the way in which knowledge about may be understood to be combined in our relation with God.

The sharp distinction between the language of science (reason) and the language of emotion is attacked by the "square" who describes life in Flatland. Usually he is an ardent, at times even Machiavellian, defender of the status quo in his two-dimensional native land. He relates that the women of Flatland abound in emotion but lack reason, and consequently they are deprived of the opportunity for an education. But he disagrees with this policy.

As things now are, we Males have to lead a kind of bi-lingual, and I may almost say bi-mental existence. With Women, we speak of "love," "duty," "right," "wrong," "pity," "hope," and other irrational and emotional conceptions, which have no existence, and the fiction of which has no object except to control feminine exuberances; but among ourselves, and in our books, we have an entirely different vocabulary and I may almost say idiom. "Love" then becomes "the anticipation of benefits"; "duty" becomes "ne-

---

[23] Langer, *Philosophy in a New Key,* p. 218. See her *Feeling and Form* (New York: Scribner's, 1956) and *Problems of Art* (New York: Scribner's, 1957) for a development of this theory and application of it to other art forms.

cessity" or "fitness"; and other words are correspondingly transmuted.[24]

This is very much like the distinction between scientific and emotive language in contemporary thought, except that the attempt to translate the emotive language into scientific equivalents has been completely abandoned.

The inseparability of feeling and knowledge is also suggested by Gordon W. Allport, who asserts that knowledge is involved in every emotional state. He illustrates:

In reality every emotional state is freighted with knowledge. Take two such elementary passions as terror and anger. The distinction between them, odd though it seems, is largely cognitive in character, for the bodily changes in both are virtually identical. In terror we know we are trapped; in anger we figure we have a fighting chance.[25]

Now the experiences that Allport mentions as examples are not encounters, but the kind of knowledge involved in them is very similar to that involved in encounter. It may not be relational knowledge, but it is certainly existential knowledge rather than objective knowledge. It is not the kind of knowledge that one would systematize into a standard of belief to be used as a test for membership in the Adventurers' Club. It is not dogmatic, objective knowledge, nor is it the product of later rational reflection. Rather, it is a personal, existential knowledge relative to one's historical situation.[26]

It is the contention of this study that encounter theology

[24] Edwin A. Abbott, *Flatland*, (5th rev. ed.; New York: Barnes & Noble, 1963), p. 52.
[25] *The Individual and His Religion* (New York: Macmillan, 1950), p. 16.
[26] For a discussion of the positive nature of historical relativism and how this necessitates, rather than invalidates, the tasks of theology and metaphysics, see Gordon D. Kaufman, *Relativism, Knowledge, and Faith* (Chicago: University of Chicago Press, 1960).

has rightly rejected propositional theology's dichotomy of objective truth or no truth, but that it has wrongly offered us another dichotomy, viz. either encounter with or knowledge about God. Although I am in basic agreement with encounter theology, I feel that it has drawn the line too sharply here. Encounter includes knowledge rather than produces knowledge only through subsequent rational reflection upon the encounter.

There is no pure encounter (i.e., unmediated by propositions). The occurrence of what we might term "nonveridical encounters" demonstrates the role of interpretation *in*, not subsequent to, encounter. For example,[27] sensing another person's presence I may speak to him, unaware that he has quietly slipped out of the room thinking that I was asleep. Again, I may sense another's excitement, and being unaware of a personal crisis which has produced nervous tension, I may interpret the excitement as the product of good fortune. Finally, something that another tells me or that I see him do may be sufficient to produce a major adjustment in my previous understanding of the other person. It is possible to be mistaken in encounter, and no matter how rare such mistakes may be (if indeed they are rare), these mistakes indicate that knowledge about another person is always involved in encounter, even if merely implicitly. Our encounter with another person is structured in terms of the knowledge about him that we have. Just as the same emotional experience may, on the basis of the cognitive element, be terror or anger, similarly the same experience in encounter may, on the basis of the cognitive element, be interpreted as joyous enthusiasm or nervous tension. Encounter is a process that *includes* interpretation, not simply provides a basis for later interpretation.

The principle that experience and interpretation must coincide is applied to the theological sphere in this reflection of

[27] For the following three examples and their significance I am indebted to Hepburn, *Christianity and Paradox*, pp. 34-38.

Bendrix, one of the chief characters in Graham Greene's novel *The End of the Affair*. "Hatred seems to operate the same glands as love: it even produces the same actions. If we had not been taught how to interpret the story of the Passion, would we have been able to say from their actions alone whether it was the jealous Judas or the cowardly Peter who loved Christ?" [28] Later, the same principle becomes relevant in his reaction to Sarah's determination to bring their affair to an end. He had interpreted her action as a rejection of him, but when he discovered Sarah's diary (Book Three) he learned that her action was an expression of her continuing love. What he had not known before was that Sarah, believing that he was killed and not simply stunned by the bomb dropped on them during an air raid, had vowed that she would give Bendrix up if God would restore him to life. The discovery of this information forced him to reinterpret all her subsequent actions and their significance for her attitude toward him. And Greene is also making this a revelation to his reader as well as to Bendrix, for it is by revealing this information that Greene hopes to enable his reader to see the hand of God in the "coincidences" of the final book of the novel.

A diary can provide important information for the understanding of death as well as of life. The Italian poet and novelist Cesare Pavese was awarded the Strega Prize, Italy's highest literary award. Shortly afterward he committed suicide. Why? In looking for an explanation two types of disappointment were most commonly mentioned. Some attributed the suicide to his disillusionment with the Communist Party; others to his broken love affair with an American movie star. However, the superficiality of such short-term explanations became obvious when a whole new dimension was brought into the picture with the publication of his private diaries covering

[28] (New York: Viking Press, 1951), p. 29.

the years from 1935 to 1950, the year of his death. These were published posthumously in 1952 as *Il Mestiere di Vivere* and translated into English by A. E. Murch in 1961 as *The Burning Brand*. Propositional knowledge is no substitute for the personal knowledge gained through encounter, but it can be a valuable supplement and corrective.

Encounter is not simply a process of relating to another person but of relating and interpreting the relation. In encounter we do not merely relate to another person but also know him on the basis of this relation. Without interpretation there is no basis for the mutual self-giving involved in encounter. Moreover, interpretation is necessary before we recognize the encounter as an I-Thou relation. There is no sense of "I" and "Thou" involvement until there is interpretation, since prior to interpretation "I" and "Thou" are indistinguishable. For example, a person who is being burned may be unable at the moment to distinguish between his perception of excruciating pain and his interpretation of this as an experience of being burned by fire. The sensing and interpreting are inseparable elements of the same experience, even though later reflection upon the experience is able to distinguish between them. In addition, the interpretation of the experience as that of being burned by fire is dependent upon prior knowledge about the nature and effects of fire.

Similarly, our sense of relation with God and our interpretation of this in terms of the resources we have in the Bible and in the various forms of the proclamation of the church are inseparably involved in our encounter with God. Faith which is exercised in complete disregard of knowledge, if there be such faith, is merely blind and meaningless faith, not trust. Interpretation is not inimical but essential to encounter with God. Encounter is not free of but dependent on I-It elements.

Personal, existential knowledge, without lessening its distinction from impersonal knowledge, is nonetheless amenable to some degree of systematic examination, and it has even been suggested that it is an appropriate item to include in a curriculum.

Philip H. Phenix contends that the area comprising such concerns as "personal knowledge" (Michael Polanyi) and the "I-Thou" relation (Martin Buber) should be included as a new branch of the curriculum for general education.[29] He coins the term "Synnoetics" to refer to this realm of meaning. This comes from the Greek *synnoesis,* meaning "meditative thought" and compounded from the roots *syn* (with, together) and *noesis* (cognition).[30] This term emphasizes the intersubjectivity of this kind of knowledge, although it may include relations to oneself and things as well as to other persons. Its main distinction from other methods of knowing is that it necessitates engagement rather than detachment. Phenix recognizes that personal knowledge is primarily a product of human association rather than formal instruction, and he recognizes the difficulties involved in dealing with this area, but he contends nonetheless that it can benefit and develop through the theoretical examination and insights of persons who have cultivated an expertise in this realm.[31] Specialization in the realm of personal knowledge benefits from the resources of philosophy, religion, psychology, and the arts (especially literature), all of which include this kind of understanding at

[29] *Realms of Meaning* (New York: McGraw-Hill, 1964), chap. 16.

[30] *Ibid.,* pp. 7, 193-94. The six realms of meaning are: Symbolics which comprises the activities of expressing and communicating (ordinary language, mathematics, and nondiscursive symbolic forms); Empirics which comprises the activities of describing (physical science, biology, psychology, and social science); Esthetics which comprises the activities of making and perceiving significant objects (music, the visual arts, the arts of movement, and literature); Synnoetics which comprises the activities of entering into relation (personal knowledge); Ethics which comprises the activities of deciding between right and wrong (moral knowledge); and Synoptics which comprises the activities of comprehending integrally (history, religion, and philosophy).

[31] *Ibid.,* pp. 196-97.

some point, although they also employ impersonal knowledge.

The proposal of this study, then, is that an existential, personal type of knowledge is present in our encounter with God, and that this knowledge is an objective basis of doctrine. This knowledge is not infallibly communicated by divine fiat but is received through human interpretation of divine confrontation. This knowledge is later elaborated into doctrine and is supplemented by the cumulative witness of the church, by rational reflection upon the encounter, and by the knowledge gained through other rational activities, such as philosophy and science. Thus we see that knowledge is operative prior to, within, and subsequent to, the encounter itself. Revelation yields doctrine, but not infallibly nor exclusively as in propositional theology. And yet revelation includes I-It elements which are elaborated into doctrines, rather than giving rise to I-It elements through subsequent rational reflection, as in the unemended form of encounter theology.

To distinguish further this existential knowledge which is the basis of trust in our proposed emendation, from the propositional knowledge which propositional theologians deem essential to trust, let us consider an illustration given by Carnell. He speaks of a letter received by Robert from his beloved, Wilma. He points out that others may read the letter, but only Robert can perceive it as a vehicle of Wilma's soul. He then adds:

But Wilma's letter is more than a medium of confrontation; it is also a propositional revelation of her will. Wilma sends her love, but she also asks Robert to meet her at the railroad station. Her words *command* as well as charm; they *communicate* as well as affect. Were Robert to rush to the airport, rather than to the railroad station, he would fail as a lover.[32]

[32] Edward John Carnell, *The Case for Orthodox Theology* (Philadelphia: Westminster, 1959), p. 34.

I would add to this that Wilma's request that Robert meet her at the railroad station is not itself encounter but provides the possibility of encounter. Robert may fail as a lover by rushing to the airport, but he may also fail as a lover at the railroad station. In propositional theology the doctrine or proposition *is* revelation. In encounter theology the doctrine or proposition *points* to revelation and hence must be subject to critical evaluation in the light of revelation. For example, Wilma may ask Robert to meet her at the railroad station, but the time interval between her departure and arrival may suggest air travel. Further investigation may discover that there is no train arriving at this time from Wilma's place of departure. In such a case Robert does not prove his love and devotion by insisting on following Wilma's instructions to the letter and showing up at the railroad station, when the total revelation suggests that the airport is more likely to have been intended. But in any case proper interpretation of Wilma's request and Robert's physical presence at her arrival are not encounter but are the basis on which encounter is possible.

Carnell's illustration also raises a question which is vital to this discussion. Can encounter occur on the basis of a written record, or must two persons be in one another's physical presence for encounter to occur? The answer defended here is that it is not absolutely essential that two persons be physically present to one another for encounter to occur, and that mediation through the written or spoken word can serve as a basis for encounter with another person who is not physically present to us. This is the basis on which encounter with God can be mediated through the biblical witness to Jesus as the Christ. Further, in order for the Bible to become a medium of revelation, the testimony of the church, through such means as preaching, administration of the sacraments, and performance of Christian service, is essential to point men to the possibility of encounter with Jesus as the Christ through the biblical witness.

Encounter with Jesus the Christ, who is not physically pres-ent, has its analogues in encounter with men. Niebuhr re-marks: "There are no geographic or temporal limits for the self's dialogue with others. Some of the significant dialogues are carried on with heroes of the past or with a deceased parent or absent lover." [33] Although each of these examples refers to an encounter with a person who is physically absent, there seem to be degrees of absence. Let us consider them in reverse order, beginning with the least degree. In the first example, there is a temporary absence; in the second, a per-manent absence due to death; and in the third, the two partners in the dialogue have never been in each other's physical pres-ence. We can illustrate each of these from incidents in novels by Sartre. Unlike Niebuhr, Brunner, and Buber, who recognize the possibility of a mutually beneficial encounter, Sartre feels that contact between persons necessarily involves a struggle to see who can retain his freedom by taking away the other's free-dom. Whether one considers the encounter to be beneficial or threatening, then, one may contend that a person can establish relation with another who is physically absent.

Niebuhr's first example was one involving a temporary ab-sence of one partner of the dialogue. An example of this in Sartre is the relation between Mathieu and Marcelle. After learning that he had caused Marcelle's pregnancy, Mathieu found, even after he had left her and had gone out into the night, that "he could not escape her" and that "Marcelle's consciousness remained." [34] Physical propinquity is not es-sential to encounter.

---

[33] Reinhold Niebuhr, *The Self and the Dramas of History* (New York: Scribner's, 1955), p. 33.

[34] Jean-Paul Sartre, *The Age of Reason,* tr. by Eric Sutton (New York: Knopf, 1947), p. 21.

Niebuhr's second example involved a permanent absence due to death. According to Sartre, the gaze of another person, even after death, can continue to exert power on us. Mathieu, seeing Lola inert and lifeless, and firmly believing her to be dead (although it developed later that she was merely unconscious), was nonetheless unable to avoid becoming the object of her gaze while he was in the room with her. He found that to take things from the room while she was lying there dead was as difficult as if she were alive and watching him.[35]

Niebuhr's third example was heroes of the past. There is a case very similar to this in the writings of Sartre, except that it is a contemporary hero figure and his voice is heard over the radio. Ella, a Jewess who lived in France, had never seen Hitler but was listening to him speak over the radio from Germany. She found herself transformed by the "gaze" of Hitler, as if the two of them were alone in the room.[36] For Niebuhr and Sartre, hearing, or even hearing about another person, may provide sufficient basis for his existential presence if he is presented through such media in a manner that enables us to share with him as a person, as a Thou.

In analogous manner the Bible and the witness of the church may present Jesus Christ to us in such a way that it is possible for us to encounter him as a Thou. Indeed, without some such mediation it would be impossible for us to encounter him. An important difference, however, is that Jesus Christ confronts us through the proclamation of the kerygma, through the work of the Holy Spirit. There is no parallel to this in the "natural" encounter as there are parallels for Jesus Christ, the kerygma, and the one who encounters Jesus Christ through this witness. The witness of the Bible and of the church make it possible for us to encounter the contemporary Christ. In

[35] *Ibid.,* pp. 248-49.
[36] Jean-Paul Sartre, *The Reprieve,* tr. by Eric Sutton (New York: Knopf, 1947), pp. 321-22.

his usual forceful style, Kierkegaard says: "Every man can be contemporary only with the age in which he lives—and then with one thing more: with Christ's life on earth; for Christ's life on earth, sacred history, stands for itself alone outside history." [37] The encounter with the eternally contemporary Christ is not simply and solely a relation with a "pure Thou," unmediated and unaccompanied by I-It elements (whatever that might be). Rather the admixture of I-Thou and I-It elements is characteristic of encounter between God and man just as it is of the encounter between man and man. The rational reflection of theology may be in a different mode, but it is not radically different; and theological activity enhances and supplements, rather than distorts, the encounter with God. We are in relation to a personal Presence and also to an existential, personal kind of knowledge. This knowledge is basic to our later rational reflection upon encounter with God. Propositions are not infallibly imparted by God, but they are an essential element, implicitly if not explicitly, prior to, during, and subsequent to, the process of revelation as encounter. It is this fullness of the encounter with God that we refer to when we speak of encountering truth.

---

[37] Sören Kierkegaard, *Training in Christianity,* tr. by Walter Lowrie (Princeton: Princeton University Press, 1944), p. 68. Cf. pp. 9, 101-2, 104, 105, 109, 171, 204.

Index